"Right" Said Fred

Building a great coaching business:
Lessons from a Master Coach

"Right" Said Fred

Building a great coaching business:
Lessons from a Master Coach

Neil Espin

Published by MVP 2007

My Voice Publishing
Unit 1 16 Maple Road
EASTBOURNE
BN23 6NY
United Kingdom

www.myvoicepublishing.com

Published by MVP April 2007

© Neil Espin 2007

Neil Espin asserts the moral right to
be identified as the author of this work

Cover design: Lisa Snape
Design: ALS Designs
ISBN 978-0-9554692-1-3

A huge thank you to;

Tracy Turmel for test driving the book in its first draft.

Lawrence Evans, Neil Davidson and Sarah Urquhart for their feedback and testimonials.

Lisa Snape for her extraordinary patience in the design and co-ordination.

Each and every one of my clients and coaches who unwittingly laid the seed for "Right" said Fred.

And to Vicki who supports me always.

"In matters of business take this as a maxim, that it is not enough to give things their beginning, direction or impulse; we must also follow them up and never slacken our efforts until they are brought to a conclusion"
Francesco Guicciardini (1483 – 1540)

A Personal Message to you

I want to say thank you; unusual before you have bought this book I know. None the less, that's what I want to do. My reason is straightforward. You could have picked up another book to help you achieve what you want to do in coaching, but you didn't. You picked up this one. I sincerely invite you to go the next step and walk over to the cashier and make this purchase. I also wish to say thank you for taking this step, not just because you made the purchase but because when you buy any book, you are putting your trust in the author, in so much as you believe you will take something from the text that you will want and need.

Neil

Contents

	Page
Introduction	13

1. Getting Started – Doing it Right — 17

2. Image and self projection for the professional coach — 31

3. How to build your contact database — 41
- 300 is your goal
- Letters that work
- Focus your marketing efforts
- Networking events
- Your professional network
- Public speaking made easy
- Referrals

4. So, why does my telephone weigh a ton? — 67

5. Preparing for the business meeting — 83
- A different approach for coaches

6. The business meeting — 91
- Your product and its fee structure
- How much should you charge?

7. Following the business meeting — 111
- Proposal template

8. So you want to increase you turnover?   121
- Puncturing the myths

9. Structuring your coaching and setting   133
    up the relationship for success

10. Accelerating your business   141
- Maintaining your efforts
- What happens if you hit the wall
  and how to avoid it
- Controlling your responses

11. New research   155

12. "Right" said Fred   161
- Empowering and limiting beliefs
- Life's lessons
- Take a 7 day detox

13. Appendices   189
- The Price is Right – Solution
- Suggested Reading List for Executive
  Coaches
- Extracts from the Film Rudy.
- An interview with Neil Espin (the Author)
- Inspirational verse
- The Duel.
- What matters the most is how you see
  yourself

Introduction

The single biggest fear for most people who are starting out on their own can often be, "I'm on my own now. Where do I start?"

This book is aimed at giving you a flying start. It is jam packed with practical things that if you choose to put into practice will actually work.

A new coach needs the opportunity and time to establish his/her professionalism and their ability to successfully work with an organisation's management team. This can be portrayed as complicated but I firmly believe that it isn't as complicated as many people would have you believe.

"Coaching is the universal language of change and learning... and values, cultural complexity and difference"

CNN

I will share a piece of information with you. You will not know this of course, but having purchased this book you will have helped me to quieten down 'Fred'.

And who is this guy Fred?

He is the guy who is brought into many aspects and situations in this book and you will find out where and how to deal with your Fred, as you move through the various chapters. We all have our own version of Fred and yes that means you too!

Now, Fred – my internal dialogue – has been telling me for a while now that I haven't the time to write a book. At times, he has told me I couldn't possibly to do it either and even if I did who the heck would want to buy it anyway? I mean who would want to hear from me? Now, rationally I know that Fred is not giving me factual information and that his statements are just not true. I know this because thousands of people have heard me speak about coaching and I have had great feedback from both open programmes and those designed to run inside organisations. The very best testimonials I receive are organisations continue to invite me back to hear more.

I have developed a successful business for myself, not once but three times. In between I have built successful operations for blue chip companies before I decided that I just wasn't put on this earth to be an employee.

The Corporate and Executive Coaching Organisation Ltd. (or CECO as it is better known) is the business I currently own, manage and founded with my co director and wife Vicki. Between us we have over 32 years coaching experience inside organisations. Along with all the tutorials we have done, I reckon this puts us firmly in the forefront of executive coaching in the UK and probably Europe.

I know what you may be thinking,

"So just how does this impact me.? "What's in this for me (or WIIFM)?"

The benefits of this experience and sustainability to you are simply this. What you are about to read is from practical knowledge of what works and what doesn't. I will identify the most common pitfalls and show you how to avoid them. The likelihood is that I have done what you are about to do, or are currently doing.

The principals in this book are not based on academia; they are certainly not theoretical and are most definitely not book-learnt. I understand that you may want to adapt some of the principals to match your own unique style but the basic ideas are a core foundation for you to work with.

The whole basis of this book is;

- To keep things simple

- To take the easy path rather than attempt to push water up hill with a stick.

- Simple and practical examples and ideas to help you succeed.

As one participant on a programme said.

"If you want to learn in a short space of time what it took Neil 30 years to figure out, and have some fun at the same time, go on one of his programmes."
Peter Law M.D Media Foundry

But be aware, this book comes with a health warning.

It is written in plain language and it will blow away many myths and enable you to understand how things made complex can be really quite simple.

This book is about the simple way for coaches to gain clients. All the intricacies, ('smoke and mirrors' that surround building a business and 'selling' your services) have been stripped away. The intention is that you will understand what you need to do without having to spend your time and money on attending sales courses.

I invite you again to read on but remember...

You have been warned!

P.S. Bye Bye Fred!

Chapter 1
Getting Started – Doing it Right

Ensure your business is built on firm foundations!

Ok, so here are a couple of scenarios that you might just be able to relate to.

You have decided to take a new career step to build yourself a new life. You figure that as you have been in business for many, or even just a few successful years, you will use this knowledge to launch yourself into the world of coaching by building your own coaching practice. By the way this used to be called a coaching business. My feeling is that we should refer to your business as a business because by doing so you will put a different emphasis on your activities and how you view yourself as a successful business person. I assume that because you are reading this book the business you are building is in coaching and to be precise, executive coaching.

You may have taken a redundancy, or have been made redundant, and have chosen to see the great opportunity that now lies before you in the next phase of your life. There is a well worn saying that springs to mind. "This is the first day of the rest of my life" and oh boy it is so true. I know it is true for me because I chose to look at life in just that way and have never ever looked back, except perhaps in disbelief that it took me so long to come to realise that I hadn't taken the amazing leap into this world of freedom before. You may of course have decided that you want personal freedom and have chosen to set up your own business, or perhaps you want a new direction in your career. Maybe you are just returning to work, there are countless reasons; however, I am certain of one thing:

The question many people ask, having decided to take the leap (and sometimes it can be a leap of faith in your own abilities) is "where on earth do I begin?" The routes into coaching can seem endless and so varied, with dozens of people offering so much advice (often conflicting) that it can be very confusing. Throughout this book my aim is to bring a little clarity and to illuminate the process you may choose to go through.

Option 1.
You can read a few books to understand the basic coaching frameworks and just get on with it. Coaching is just about asking questions in a structured way and nodding in the right places, isn't it?

I mean, how difficult can asking a few questions be?

Option 2.
Hmm! This doesn't seem enough somehow. Perhaps I should listen to some audio on this, but then who do I listen to? None the less, you choose who you think will help you, now you are ready to get clients. By the way these used to be called customers. After all, if the

authors and published coaches can do it then so can you, right? Wrong!

So many published experts can write about the subject, (some can't even do that and use ghost writers). Some can even talk about the subject. However the key question is can they actually coach? Believe me some just can't.

There is one organisation in the UK that has become the largest coach training school in the UK. Our organisation CECO, were contracted by this organisation for five years to tutor, act as a quality control, write and deliver the courses that were offered at that time, as well as being platform speakers on life coaching and our speciality, executive coaching. To enable us to be in this position we had been coaching for many years before this organisation opened its doors. However without doubt we feel that by working with this company we did our part in helping to put the term coaching on the map in the UK.

Great coaches are hard to find and the trouble with great coaches once you find them, is that they tend to make coaching look simple. Here is the rub. If you are familiar with the learning curve, the great coaches are at the level of unconscious competence. This means they are good at what they do and they don't need to think about it anymore. It's something they now do naturally. The steps before this ultimate stage of development are;

Unconscious Incompetence, i.e
I don't know what I don't know. Therefore this looks easy. Let me at it!

Conscious Incompetence, i.e.

I now know what I don't know, I am now learning something new about this and I am not sure I can do it. Don't be surprised if your learning and even your confidence takes a dip in this stage. Its normal and all part of your personal growth to the next stage, which is

Conscious Competence, i.e.

I now know that I am good at this and I know why. I may have to think about it but that works for me. You may even think that you sound a little wooden and the coaching isn't flowing how you would like it to. Focusing on this is the last thing you need to do. Your client probably won't even notice. They will be too occupied processing and answering the question you have just asked them. Trust yourself until you get to the next stage, which is of course

Unconscious Competence, i.e.

I am good at this and I don't have to think about it anymore. It just becomes a natural state to be in. I certainly find that sometimes I may not feel ready to coach. However as soon as I meet my client, it is like throwing a switch and the coaching just begins to flow all the time, every time. I never question this or ask why it is so, it just works. Always. It will for you once you are at this stage of your development.

Here is a little tip for you. If you are tired and facing a long drive home push yourself back to Conscious Competence, remember how to drive and the process that you have been taught. Typically, mirror, signal, manoeuvre, accelerate and watch your speed. In other words ensure you think about what you need to do whilst driving to stay safe and the chances are you will. This also applies in many areas of life, including your coaching.

The reason great coaches work at Unconscious Competence is because they didn't do what you may be about to do. Great coaches did not start life as 'rogue coaches'.

Hey who are you calling a rogue coach?

Ok! A rogue coach is someone who, in terms of learning the art of coaching, only read a book, at best At worst they used to be a trainer, consultant or mentor until they realised pretty quickly that coaching is the fastest form of developing people and is a hot topic. Therefore, by simply changing the title on a business card to Coach they can get an increase in their business and in turn, an increase in their revenue.

B. C. McGraw Hill Education states;

'Many Industry sources now state that the global business demands for coaching is almost doubling each year'

Not a bad business to be in is it, if you are great at what you do.

This is further backed up by **The Harvard Business Report** which states;

'In the USA the estimated spend on Executive Coaching is $1billion p.a.'

It is anticipated that in the UK the spend on Executive Coaching in The City alone is estimated at £40 million p.a. So here in the UK we still have a way to go. I often hear the same question on opportunity and amount of available business from new coaches.

"When will we reach saturation point?"

Looking at the above figures, I reply:
"I wouldn't even concern yourself with this at all. Become a great coach and you will probably never need to worry about a lack of opportunity."

Please don't learn the tricks of the trade. Simply learn the trade.

So the rogue coach hasn't even invested time in learning the basics of the profession, or the underlying principals of what coaching actually is. They may think, "I know the GROW model" or to look smart, "I have made up my own coaching model. This will be my USP" (unique selling point).Not a great start is it? After all, the GROW model is the most well known and certainly the most effective model I have come across in all my years as an Executive Coach.

Here is an example, so you don't fall into the same trap. I met a business leader who recounted this tale to me.

"I drive to London to meet my coach I sit and talk to the coach who religiously writes down what I say, never asks me any questions or challenges what I say and what I need in order to achieve my aims. I do this for an hour and then drive back a round trip of 350miles. What do you think?"

My reply was

"Is this helping you achieve your aims and objectives, because if it isn't, then I'm not sure what it is, but it sure isn't coaching?"

I gave a 30 minute taster coaching session there and then and he asked:

"What was that?"

"Coaching" I said.

You won't be surprised to learn that it was very different and challenging. I gained the business.

So the coach in the example is not you, and it never will be, will it? In addition to reading and so on, you have decided to attend a comprehensive training programme, not just a course, and you have invested your hard earned income, as well as time to ensure you get the best possible grounding in coaching, and probably even an accreditation to give you that little extra confidence and a huge amount of credibility.

Congratulations. This puts you in the top 3%-4% of people in this country who are prepared to take on this form of personal development. This is a staggeringly low percentage of people who are actually prepared to invest in their own professional development. Are you feeling better? You should be.

You are on the right track and ready to think about the next stage. Here are a few key points that you need to be satisfied on before selecting your training provider;

• Ensure your training company of choice is well recognised and gives you a full account of what you can expect in return for your custom and investment.

• Ensure the tutors are successful coaches, are credible and can walk the talk.

• Ensure your aftercare to protect your investment is comprehensive, tangible and is in place. Test it out.

• Ensure the organisation can answer all your questions. This will count when you are working with your clients/customers and the inevitable questions you will face from them and you may just need some help with answering.

• Ensure there is someone who can answer these questions with experience and authority. You simply must have access to someone who understands the issues you face away from a classroom and can answer them for you or in true coaching style help you find your own solutions.

- Accreditation will count when you are talking to prospective organisations who will want to know that you can coach and have been professionally trained.

- How is this accreditation recognised? Is it self appointed by the training organisation or has it been recognised by an external organisation?

The professionals inside organisations with whom you are looking to do business might not ask you outright about your credentials; however purchasers of executive coaching are not easily fooled by expensive looking brochures, gloss and clever sales techniques.

You will find when you are obtaining business that organisations in the main are well past the novelty of 'wow what is coaching?' It is now more along the lines of 'Coaching? So what? I receive a dozen calls a day from people trying to sell me coaching'. You need a different approach to stay ahead of the game and to keep your company and your offering fresh and vibrant. If you want to know more about this and understand the "what" as well as the "how", read on.

Finally, in this section I want to make you aware of the high level of time and energy some people put into achieving degrees in coaching. Whilst I believe there is a place for this and I understand some people enjoy the academic side of things, it can on occasion be taken too far.

An example of this is;

A Head of Learning and Development in a global organisation has achieved a Degree in Coaching. During our discussion, I asked the question:

"This is great for the company and you. So how many clients do you have?"

He replied,

"Clients? I don't have clients. I just write about it. I can't actually do it"

There is nothing wrong with this at all and I am not judging this particular person. However I do feel it is unprofessional for a coach who has gone down this route and can't coach, to set themselves up as a guru or platform speaker on what is, after all a practical subject.

On a separate note, you may also find that coaches, who are published and acclaimed, actually begin to believe their own publicity and PR. They seem to stop doing the things that got them recognised in the first place. When this happens they can very quickly lose touch with the latest thinking, the practice of being in front of clients asking questions and really listening to the answers on a regular basis. If this happens, then how will they be able to help you, whether you are a new coach or an experienced coach looking for further professional development?

The phrase so often heard in coaching and is certainly true for me is;

The hardest work you will ever do is on yourself.

Twelve Key Steps to Establish Credibility as a Corporate Coach

I am often asked by coaches. "What is it that you do that makes it easy for you to gain credibility with organisation. And when you are working with these organisations how do you manage to stay there?" The answer to this question is not particularly straightforward, in that it takes many of the things that I will cover in this book. However in a nutshell I have detailed twelve key skills or habits that will help you with your business and your clients.

1. Keep abreast of hot business topics/challenges.

Subscribe to business magazines and free papers, like the Harvard Business Review

2. Get to grips with the culture quickly.

Always be on the look out when in an organisation for tell tale signs of how the organisation operates. Don't just sit in reception; look at the company newsletter and talk to the receptionists. They are a mine of useful information.

3. Maintain active consciousness of the level of your coaching capacity and then consistently take action to lift it even higher.

Invest in yourself. Continue to develop through your networks and ask for feedback from coaches you respect.

4. Establish a clear contract with the organisation and with each client.

See chapter 10

5. Develop a deep understanding of key coaching issues for people in organisations and build a toolkit of relevant business models.

If you are looking for a toolkit that has been developed and in constant use by successful and experienced coaches, then log onto **www.cecoach.com**

6. Continually raise your own self awareness through client feedback.

Ask your clients how you are performing as a coach. At the end of every session, you will soon establish the areas that you are great at and those that are development points.

7. Maintain a strong link with your own mentor coach.

If you don't have one then find one. A mentor coach is invaluable. This needs to be someone who can coach the coach, and who will have a wealth of experience to help guide you to business success.

8. Corporate life and organisations are about people - so know that everything you've learned so far about coaching people is absolutely relevant to coaching in the corporate environment.

You do not come to coaching as a blank sheet of paper. You have been in training for this role your whole life.

9. Raise your understanding of the corporate context with particular emphasis on learning and using corporate language.

Search out a book that will give you a glossary of terms that are used inside organisations. This will enable you to understand and use business language.

10. Be passionately clear about the difference between coaching and other ways of developing people.

Know what coaching is and isn't. Have a clear definition in your mind about the key differences. Keep it simple.

11. Identify key stakeholders and focus on satisfying their needs.

Work out who has a stake in the coaching you are doing. Ensure you communicate with them and manage their expectations. Look for people with a high level of influence rather than importance.

12. Consistently demonstrate your understanding that impact on bottom line performance is critical to the success of coaching by strongly encouraging your clients to establish clear measures of success.

This is covered in chapter twelve. If in doubt use the Kirkpatrick model of measurement.

Level 1 – gain the reaction of your client

Level 2 – ask the client if they are gaining knowledge and skills

Level 3 – notice any changes in the client's behaviour

Level 4 – what is the impact on the business?

Chapter 2
Image and self projection for the professional coach

This topic may seem obvious to many people but I cannot stress enough at this stage, the importance of getting this right and the disaster that will ensue if you get it wrong. In fact, if you do get it wrong, (whatever that means) you may not get the business and you will always wonder why. Just stop and think about it, how many clients will tell you

"It was down to the fact I didn't like the way you looked and acted when you came to see me?"

Very few, I suspect. Most people are simply too polite to say this to another human being. Don't give them the opportunity.

I have met thousands of potential coaches and many others on a more personal level who have come through CECO's own open executive coaching programme. The area of image and projection is probably the biggest single area that raises discussion and often the temperature. Why? Well, let's face it. We are addressing how you look, what you do, how you act and what you sound like. It's hardly surprising the temperature can rise somewhat as this is highly personal and may challenge your views about yourself. Therefore, let me state that this is an opinion based on years of working in the corporate market place, both as a senior manager inside blue chip organisations, (yes, I have been on the other side of the desk making decisions about suppliers) as well as an executive coach and presenter. The choice, to take heed of the views that I express, as always is yours. I cannot however resist the following phrase,

You never get a second chance to make a first impression...

The facts on image are almost identical to those on communication; first impressions are made within the first few seconds of someone seeing you for the first time. The following percentages are always in play, both in business and socially.

First Impressions are based on;

> 55% on how you look
> 38% on what you do
> 7% on what you say

So, words are important, but not as important as how you look and what you do. If you are going to say something in the first moments of a meeting, then keep it brief and make sure what you say is not vital to you achieving the business. Both you and the client need to settle into the discussion first as you begin weigh each other up and build a rapport. It may surprise you to know that some buyers are just as nervous as the person who is offering a service or product. Prior to meeting some buyers, I have been given 'the low down' on them and have been told they are difficult, hard nosed and a cold fish.

After meeting them, I have given feedback to the person who gave me the information and said.

"Nothing of the sort. We got on really well. What a great person they are" much to the amazement of the receiver.

So what is the client/customer looking for in this area that makes up 55% of the 1st impression? They are looking at you. How many of you have interviewed as part of your role? How many have bought anything of significance? All of you, I'll wager. You have done what your potential client is doing.

Think of something you didn't buy. Did you like the product or service you were purchasing? But you were not quite sure what it was that made you not buy and walk away. Consciously, or sub consciously, it was something to do with the person who was dealing with you that turned you away. That is down to first impressions. How quickly did you make your mind up about the person you were dealing with? Then you spent the next hour convincing your self that you were right? Admit it, you did.

To begin to understand why we act in this way, we need to look at our childhood messages about people and indeed things, such as;

- Look before you leap
- Beauty is only skin deep
- All that glitters is not gold
- Don't judge a book by its cover

Except, we do tend to judge a book by the cover. Recall the last time you were in a bookshop and you wanted a book, but had nothing in mind. What was it that attracted you to certain books? Maybe you knew the author or maybe you liked the cover of the book? We spend so much time seeking information that we loose the skill of the 'hunch'. How many great business ideas have never come to fruition because the numbers didn't seem to add up, or it was felt that there wouldn't be a demand? Just like the guy who turned down the Beatles and the rest, of course, is history.

Mind you, as an operational manager for many years, part of my role was to have the final say in recruiting my own managers. I think I must have been a nightmare to interview with because I asked myself just three simple questions;

Do I like you?

Can I get on with you?

Will you do a good job for me?

Of course the HR professionals had carried out screening and testing, asked competency based questions and so on and there I was asking just three simple questions. I was going on a hunch and you know what? I feel I got it right more often than not.

Harvard Business Review published a paper on decision making with the bottom line findings being ;

The person who always takes risks and is not risk averse generally makes 2 big mistakes a year;

The person who never takes a risk and is risk averse generally makes 2 big mistakes a year.

"This should give you confidence!"

The three questions I had in my mind mattered the most to me and the answers I was searching for inevitably swung the job offer one way or the other. Someone, you, may be absolutely perfect for the client as their coach in terms of ability, but if the client doesn't like you, then what?

Malcolm Gladwell in his book 'Blink' refers to the part of our brain that jumps to conclusions as 'the adaptive unconscious' and goes on to say it is the most important new field in psychology. What conclusion can we draw from this? To my mind it's a simple phrase that most people know but is often forgotten.

"People buy people first"

So the real deal here is this. It really does matter what impression you make in the first few seconds. Therefore it is about how you look and what you do.

However, I can hear dozens of coaches saying,

"I am intending to work in manufacturing, or marketing, or the leisure industry. The clients dress down and don't wear business dress and I want to blend in"

Here is a different view. I don't want you to blend in. I want you to stand out and be exactly what you are: a professional coach. When I see the professionals who work with us, (our suppliers) I want them to look professional. Its part of what I pay fees for.

Do you need more convincing? Ok then; here is a real example of a coach getting it wrong, big time.

CECO are doing business with a major organisation and we deal with the HR Director. The Learning and Development manager had experience of another coaching organisation and wanted the HR Director to meet with them. He did, and this is the feedback we received.

"I didn't like the coach after the first few minutes. he didn't even have the courtesy to wear a tie, just a jacket, trousers and tee shirt. If he had done any research at all he would have known I am a stickler for appearance. As he didn't bother, after that everything that was said seemed a little dishevelled. You were never in any danger of losing our business. Not only do you do a first class job, you always respect us as customers in the way you and your team turn out. We like to deal with professionals. Thank you."

The key message I am driving home is this. If in doubt always dress to impress in business dress. It does count. Small point, isn't it, or is it? You decide.

Having looked at how you appear to others, let's turn our attention to what you do to achieve the next 33% of first impressions. This is about how you walk into an office. Do you stand upright and walk in confidently,(not arrogantly), or do you hunch over and look at the floor? No guesses as to which of these has the biggest impact.

You will then probably shake hands. There are many ways to do this. Here are six common mistakes.

The dead cod. You slap a cold, clammy hand into the client's hand and give a limp handshake.

The vice. You grip the client's hand too firmly in a crushing grip. You can tell when this happens. A tear runs down the client's face and they need to go to casualty afterwards.

The water pump. You shake the client's hand like you are pumping water from a well. When their eyes start to rattle around in their head you have gone too far.

Women will break. You pay them no respect at all and gently hold a woman's finger-ends with a little and delicate handshake. They will hate you forever and want to shake you by the throat!

I'm in charge. You hold out your outstretched hand palm down. This means dominance.

You're in charge. You hold out your outstretched hand palm up. This means submission.

These are all guaranteed to put you on the back foot, so

as you are going to shake hands anyway, you may as well get it right,

We are equals. Hold out your hand on the level, thumb at the top little finger at the bottom, grip firmly and shake hands for a couple of seconds, looking at the client and say, *"Hello my name is..."* Simple, that's it. So why do so many people get it wrong?

As a trial, just notice who shakes your hand and in what way they do it. It's good fun.

After you have completed the formalities, sit comfortably and please don't dive into your briefcase at this early stage. The client may have to stand up to see where you have gone. If you do need to get something from your case then do this neatly once you have built rapport and at the appropriate time.

Do have a business card to hand. In some organisations it is the culture or the done thing to swap cards at the beginning of a meeting. Please ensure you have enough for everyone there, otherwise you have to dive into the case again.

Finally, and please don't be offended, ensure your aftershave or perfume isn't strong enough to knock over a bull elephant.

To this day, after 30 years of being in business, I still check my appearance. Do I have everything I will need? Does my pen work? And so on before every meeting. It's a good habit that serves me well.

Now you have 93% of your communication working for you and you have put yourself in the best possible position at this stage and have gained an edge over someone who doesn't do this at all. This is all about giving yourself that extra 0.5 percent in each area which all add up to a significant number in the end when the decision on who to select is made.

At last you can say something other than hello but what are you going to say? You may feel nervous. Whether you are new to this or an old hand, this is normal. Anyone who says they are not has more than likely lost that all important edge. Be positive. This nervousness enables you to perform to your best and only lasts a short time, until you are in full control of the situation. Talk adult to adult, with an even pace and tone, which does not mean dull. In the battle between your throat and diaphragm, ensure the diaphragm wins. Talk from way down with authority, rather than squeaky from the throat.

Remember to keep what you say brief and clear.

- Your name again

- Your company

- Why you are there

That's it; this is enough for the key 7% of words. After this, you want the client to talk to you and give you information.

Key messages

How you look reflects your success and who you are.

If you feel happy and enthusiastic about what you do, notify your face.

Chapter 3
How to build your contact database

As you are building your reputation, to enable you to gain business and make new contacts, word of mouth and referrals will become a life blood to your success. However it is also vital to have as many methods of generating business as you can. If you go fishing and have just one line out you can only catch one fish. If you have many lines out you have a greater chance of catching more than one. This is obvious I know, but how about launching a trawler?

I guess for most new coaches this is the point where you may feel;

"I can't do this. It's a bit scary."

"I don't know anyone who will buy my services."

My responses to you are;

"Yes, you can do this."

"Yes, you do know people who will buy your services."

I know the systems I am going to describe to you really work. How do I know this? I have done this myself, for myself and for other organisations. To prove the methods do work I am going to relate how I have coached other coaches on how to build a list of contacts, through which they have gained business. I have tutored many more coaches on the same systematic approach and they too have gained business. And in many cases from the most unlikely sources. It is not as difficult as you might think and you can do this immediately, unless you decide to put it in the 'too hard box' and trust to luck instead.

Give a man a fish he will eat for a day, teach a man to fish and he will eat forever. (Chinese proverb)

300 is your goal

This is really simple. Here's what I want you to do.

1. Just take a clean sheet of paper and divide it into 4 columns. The 4 headings are:

Family

Friends

Acquaintances – people who you give your business to or courses that you have been on, include the hosts and the delegates.

Other businesses – those that have contacted you, to do business with you. Or people you know from your time in business.

2. Write down names in the appropriate column, with as much information as possible and no editing out. My guess is that as you begin to think of people, you will start to say to yourself,

"This person can't help me" or;

"This person won't be interested "and so on...

Stop, right here, right now, no editing.

Think about it this way. Someone else will think of them as potential clients so why not let that someone be you? How annoying would it be if you edited a name out because of a preconception, only to be told later?

"Hey guess what? I have just met a great executive coach. Just what we have been looking for."

It is a bit late for you to then say lamely, *"I do that"*

Your goal is to get 300 names. This is not as many as you may think. One coach who attended our programme did it overnight. My guess is that he will succeed and was motivated to do something for himself.

I am not suggesting you coach your family or even your friends. However they can be a valuable source for gaining information. The key principle is this, whilst they might not have the decision making authority in an organisation, nine times out of ten they will know who does and can give you the contact details. A really good example of this is, a member of my family worked for a large company and not only did they know the person to contact with the authority to purchase executive coaching, they also knew the contact in one of their key suppliers.

Work out the numbers. If your family and friends each knew 3 people and you had 100 names in those 2 columns then you already have 300 contact names

Moving onto acquaintances. These are people who you give your business to. You are setting up a business, and you may have accountants, printers, web designers and so on. Again, no editing, if you get 50 names and if they each knew 3 people you now have another 150 contacts.

Your contact list is now standing at 450 contacts, from a database of 150 names.

Now all you need are another 150 names to achieve the goal of 300. Onto the last area of businesses. Who do you know from your time in business? Whose details have you still got? What is your personal network like? And so on. This should see you home with 300 names.

Once you have this you have achieved Project 300 and you will have around 750 contacts in your database. Not a bad start is it? And you thought you didn't know anybody. You also have something that others may not think of; you either know the person or can use the name of the person who recommended you, with their permission of course.

Now you have the names, what will you do with them? You can telephone, send an introductory letter, send an email or send a direct mail flyer.

All of these can work. However it seems to me that the telephone is by far the best, especially if you send a brief letter first and then follow up by telephone. I can appreciate for some this sounds scary but it's just Fred in your head. What is the worst that can happen? Probably the worst thing is that someone says no.

That won't harm you and remember, they are not saying no to you. They are saying no to the proposition. It's not personal. Equally they are not saying no forever, just at that time.

Hang on a minute. Who is this Fred chap?

Ok, for those of you who have heard me speak on this subject before you know exactly who Fred is. For those who haven't, he is the little voice that lives in your sub-conscious or unconscious mind. The one that tells you about all the things that can go wrong, the self doubt that you don't need right at the key moment.

When will Fred talk to you?
When you are about to do something for the first time.
When you are facing a challenge.
When you are about to do something important.
At 3.00am.
When you have time on your hands, like driving.
When you are about to speak in public, and so on.

So why on earth have I given this part of my mind (this voice) a name? Its so I can talk back. Here is how it goes.

Fred says;
"You will never do this"

I reply **"Fred shut up,"** but not that politely. **"Give me something positive and I will get back to you later."** I can then get on with what I am about to do.

Do it. It works.

You will discover more about Fred in Chapter 13

Letters that work

Here is a sample letter that you can adapt to your own personality and style.

Alternatively you can adapt your elevator speech, which you can find out more about in this chapter on Networking Events

Dear xxxxxxxxx

Your colleague, xxxxxx, gave me your name as she/he believes you will be interested in a unique service we offer.

We can make your existing staff training programme even more effective –or introduce new initiatives that will enhance your existing staff learning and development policy.

In fact we estimate that a unique approach to coaching people to achieve at a higher level has certainly been recognised by the business community in general. We have numerous surveys and statistics to prove this claim.

This is because when someone is coached on an ongoing basis it is proven to be far more effective than investing in training alone.Transfering learning from the classroom to the workplace is a key factor in developing people and is not always easy to do.

We know how to maximise your investment in this area.

Some of the benefits of coaching include:

- More motivated staff – especially in sales and customer facing teams
- An increase in each individual's level of performance
- The company develops a more defined sense of purpose and achievement

In today's competitive market attracting and retaining the right people has been identified as a key business imperative. A recent survey in the Times bears out this claim.

In an initial meeting with you I can gain enough information about your business and its aims to suggest a cost effective coaching programme, tailored to your requirements.

I have made a diary note to call you before the end of the week to schedule a business meeting.

I look forward to speaking with you to arrange a time to meet and to establish how we can help your business to implement one of the most powerful developmental tools in the market today.

Yours sincerely,

xxxxxxxxx

So here you have a template to develop into something bespoke for your unique approach.

Focus your marketing efforts

When you are doing this exercise you have many choices to make. You can look to become Global, European, National, or local to you. You can aim at a specific market sector to specialise in, you can aim at multinationals, large corporations SMEs,(small to medium enterprises) these are typically companies with up to 250 employees, sole traders or business start ups.There are many combinations and the choice can be bewildering. But whichever you choose, here is a principle that will help you.

The next exercise is to draw 3 interlocking circles or a 3 circle ven diagram,

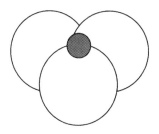

Let's say you want to work within 60 miles of your home, 1 hours drive:

  Within a retail sector
  With SMEs

You simply put each of these in a circle.

Where a contact falls into the blue area of the diagram, this becomes your prime focus.

If a contact meets 2 of your criteria they are secondary targets.

Where a contact meets just one, either leave it alone or make a conscious choice whether to do business with them. You have now made a choice from a positive position rather than chasing anything that comes along.

Now you have this focus you can ask the Chamber of Commerce to produce a disc of your key criteria and the with following information;

  MD or HR contact,
  Address,
  Telephone no.
  Web site
  Number of employees.

So now how many contacts do you have for your database? Although you might wish to say in your letter. "As a fellow member of the Chamber etc."

There are many other places you can get these listings. It's just a matter of research. So far, so good. You are now ready for the next stage, networking.

<u>Networking events</u>

Key message

At the beginning of your networking be open and honest about your intentions. You are there to gain contacts and business.

This is not as daunting as it may seem. Remember at networking events everyone is there for the same reason, to make new contacts. If however, you go with the intention of helping someone out or freely giving information, you may find that you are just a little bit different and the energy you give off will be relaxed and positive. Remember what you give out you will get back 10 fold in the long run.

So where will you go and what will you say?

As this is very likely to be the 1st time you will come into contact with potential clients, please recall the chapter on impact and 1st impressions. This is where it begins to count. You may have heard about something called an 'elevator speech', a twenty to thirty second sound bite of what you do and who you are. This needs to be precise enough to give the person who asks "what do you do?" or "where are you from?" enough information to enable them to understand your business. However, the key thing is, it should also encourage them to ask for more information. So, once you have your introduction worked out, the rest is about the contact asking questions and you answering them. Of course, you already know the answers, so you are in control. Simply ensure your answers are juicy enough to make the contact want to know more, e.g.

Give some examples of your successes.

Explain a problem one of your existing clients had and how you tackled it.

Describe a situation you are about to see a client with.

Give some clear examples of how coaching has helped organisations develop their staff.

It goes without saying that all the above are anonymous and confidential, something your contact will respect. You are looking for 6 outcomes,

1. The contact asks you to arrange a meeting

2. The contact asks you to call the person who deals with people development. Don't forget to ask if it's ok to use the contact's name

3. If they already use coaching, that's good news for you. Ask them in what areas they use it and how they measure its effectiveness. You can now ask for a business meeting to discuss how you work with your client companies

4. The contact asks. "Can you do this for my organisation?" * see below

5. At the very least, get their business card and give yours. Tell them you will contact them after the event and find out when a good time will be to make a call.

6. Finally, ask them to introduce you to someone else.

Some very important do's

Do have your diary with you.

Do have enough business cards.

Do say your company name with pride, even if you think 'but it's just me'. It doesn't matter. Its how you see yourself that counts.

Know the success of the event is not how many cards you give out. Its how many you collect.

*And finally, never ever give away a yes!

What do I mean by that?
I mean, if the client says. "Can you do this for my organisation?" and you say "yes" immediately then you have just given yes away for nothing. Then where do you have left to go? And the contact isn't any more committed to take action.

Instead, if the client says, "Can you do this for my organisation?" you say, "Would you like me to?"

The client then says "yes," and all you need to do is get out your diary and book a business meeting, job done. Easy isn't it?

All we need to do now is work out your elevator speech. The next exercise I want you to do is to list all the words or brief phrases that you think will portray you in the best way. I can't tell you what to say. However, here is a steer;

Professional

Specialist

Executive coach

Business focused

Working with organisations

Significant individual, team or organisational impact

In areas such as

- Performance
- Leadership
- Change
- Teams
- Communication

I can say with confidence that these are the big 5; the areas that I am asked to work in most frequently. If you decide to put the above together with some link words you will have a pretty good elevator speech. Do personalise it and ensure you are comfortable with it, but no editing, and do put a question at the end, such as;

Would you like an example?

What do you think about this?

What challenges do you face at the moment?

This prompts a response and you are in conversation.

That's about it. Work the room. Don't stay with one person all the time. That's not networking is it? Go for it. You are doing this for you; the very best reason you have. It's not for someone else, or an employer. The only people who benefit now are you and the contacts that become your client organisations.

Finally have another little word with Fred, and tell him you will get back to him later.

Key message
Make a follow up call or send an email thanking the people you met for their time and how interested you were. Make it a personal note. You can assume you will be the only person who does this and it will go a long way.

Remember to add all the people you meet and gain business cards from to your own community and keep in touch with them.

Your professional network

What is your professional network like? How many people do you know that can fulfil important roles for you in a professional sense? The types of roles that are useful in a professional network are;

- Gatekeepers – people who can open doors for you

- Mentors

- Innovators – people who can create innovative solutions or propositions for you

- Advisers – who do you trust and respect that you can go to for advice?

- Coaches

- Nurturers – who will put the kettle on if you are having a tough time?

- Partners – what business partnerships do you have?

- Business introducers

Networking is not all about generating immediate sales opportunities. Great networks include other professionals who are in the same profession as you, or are in complimentary professions. For example. CECO needed to help a client with a 360 degree feedback process before the executive coaching programme. We knew an expert in this field and were able to manage the entire project for the client. The benefits for the client were, we were the sole point of contact, they received just one invoice and CECO helped construct the end to end process for the client.

You never know when you may need some associate help to fulfil a large contract, or want someone with experience to coach you through the contract.

There is a view that direct mail, cold calling and letters of introduction just do not work. In my view the more pillars of success you build the stronger your business will be. However, I don't believe we can get away from the fact that Networking is by far and away the very best method of gaining business in a coaching industry.

If you don't like the network you are in or it doesn't give you what you want then think radically. Build your own networking events. Own them and lead them. This is not as difficult as you may think. All you need is a little courage and imagination to find like minded and com-plimentary businesses. Invite them to a breakfast meet-ing, by invitation only, RSVP the invite. Ensure you have a captivating theme for the meeting and follow up the invites personally. You are the main speaker, however the opportunities to network for your guests are bril-liant.

If you want to find out how to do this just visit; **www.cecoach.com**

The network you want is already there.

Key Message
The very best time to network is when you don't need to.

Public speaking made easy

I recall a saying, which makes for good reading.

When surveyed, most managers who were asked, said:

"I would rather die than stand up and speak in public."

A bit drastic for my liking!

Another old chestnut
'The human brain begins to work from the moment you are born and never stops until you stand up to speak in public.'

Is this you? If it is, then I am directly addressing you. Just answer this simple question.

What's the worst that can happen?

Embarrassment
Nerves kick in
Forgetting your lines
Blushing and feeling hot
Believing no one wants to listen to what you have to say
And so on

Begin by looking at things from a different perspective. If, and I mean if, any of the above happens, the audience might just feel for you. They are not there to pull you up or catch you out. Don't forget all of us who choose to do this had to start somewhere. As for me, I love doing it now. It's great fun. I have met some remarkable people whilst up front and had some really great fun with them. Just enjoy the ride and know that you may have just conquered a fear.

So why should you do it? In truth, you don't have to. No one is making you. It's your choice to promote yourself and your business to potential new clients. On CECO's coach training programme, we ask groups to prepare a talk overnight and present it the next day. We have heard some really innovative things, some with humour and some without. One new speaker, who had never done anything like this before, volunteered and made a great job of it.After that we couldn't get her away from the front!

So if you choose to go down this route, and I recommend that you do, here are a few very simple things you can do that will actually work.

- Tell yourself you can do this. It's just your subconscious that is telling you that you can't. You got it. Guess who has just made an appearance?

Hey, it's Fred again!

- The key to a successful talk is preparation, preparation and then of course more preparation.

- Have a strong opening and finish.

- Have great structure for your talk.

Here is one that is a standard. However, it works;

• **Tell them what you are going to tell them**
Your name
Your company name
What you do
What you will cover. Yes it's just an extended elevator speech- I believe in recycling.
When you will take questions. (This is probably best done at the end.)

• **Tell them**
- Use the words, "you", "we" and "together" in the first few minutes as often as you can. This develops a feeling of talking directly to each individual rather to thin air and it is inclusive.

- What executive coaching is?

- Your key area of speciality, if you have one.

- Identify the big 5 areas that organisations ask for help in. (You know what these are from your elevator speech).

- Facts, surveys and case studies.

- Benefits to the audience, the WIIFM (what's in it for me).

Most audiences tend to lose a little interest in the middle, so either make your key points early or later in the presentation, or put in an interactive session, for example a quiz or a discussion group.

• Tell them what you have told them
Summarise what you have said.

Put in a call to action. You want them to do something.

Inform the audience **during your talk** that you have a limited number of slots available, say 6, and you will allocate them to those people who meet with you at the end of the presentation.

Then tell them the session will be complimentary, on the basis that you can coach 1 more individual in their organisation. That extra individual needs to be a decision maker, HR professional or a key influencer. Just ensure it's someone who can help you achieve your aim, which is, of course, to do business with them.

This works on the basis of scarcity. People will always want what they think they can't have, or that someone else is getting.

Tell them you will stay at the end to arrange the client appointments.

Take questions; remember you are in control here. When you feel you have had enough, tell them just one more. This leaves the others who have a question needing to see you at the end.

Thank them and sit down. Accept the applause graciously.

• After the talk
Ask the host for a guest list.

Stay afterwards with your diary and the allotted dates for the complimentary sessions.

Remember to collect business cards.

• Preparing the talk
All you need to do now is:

Put some words around your facts and examples.

Time your talk.

Establish how you can make it interactive. You may have a small exercise you want the audience to take part in.

You may decide to coach a volunteer with a live demonstration which is impressive; this will depend on the time allocation.

If you have notes, and it is ok to have notes, put them on cards, number them and then pin the cards together. The last thing you need is to drop them on the floor and then not be able to re establish the order.

Practise, practise and then practise some more!

On the day

Arrive early to get a feel for the room.

Meet the host and establish how they will introduce you.

Find out about the audience.

Check out the room from where you will be standing, then from the sides and rear of the room. Put your energy into the space.

Become familiar with the venue,

If you choose to use a flip chart remember that you need to write in large letters in black or blue. Do it and check it out from all angles.

If you use power point please keep it brief. Your slides support what you say. They are not the presentation.

Use visuals wherever you can.

And last but not least. (That's it. You've got it,) have a word with Fred.

Strategic Alliances

This is an absolutely brilliant method of getting business, CECO currently has four of these alliances and they are working for the mutual benefit of all of us.

Search for organisations or individuals who do not offer coaching but who do offer a complimentary service, e.g.

Training companies, consultancies or management development organisations and so on. Your proposal to them is very simple. They introduce you to their clients, either under your own brand or under theirs, and you become the coaching provider for them, for an agreed percentage of the fees. As they already have a relationship with the client, this carries a lot of weight and credibility. It also gives the company you have made the alliance with, a great benefit for their business with an additional offering to their clients. The real beauty of this is very simple. You are not in competition with the company in any way, and in fact you are a terrific support to any training solution, in that you can help transfer the learning from the training to the workplace. So they don't have to stop any initiative they have underway with their clients to do business with you because you simply support it.

The following quote will help any business partner understand this;

In 1997 the International Personnel Management Association published research which compared standalone training with coaching and training combined. The research demonstrated that training alone increased productivity by 22.4% whereas training plus coaching grew productivity by an amazing 88%.

You may also benefit in terms of your fees. If the company has an agreed set of fees already in place, which fit with your expectations (after their percentage deduction) you are home and dry. If not, then set your fees and explain that you are a specialist in your field and that high quality executive coaching attracts a fee structure of (your fee structure). They can charge you out at this amount.

The key question is. "Are you prepared to work for a lower fee than expected whilst you are building your business, reputation and testimonials?" To me this is a simple one to answer. Because the alliance will be marketing your services there is little financial risk to you and yet maximum exposure. Therefore you may decide, 'Yes I am prepared to enter into this arrangement'.

Alliances do work. It's as simple as that.

Referrals

There is much written about referrals and how to get them. Instead I much prefer to keep it simple (and effective).

When you have completed a piece of work, or your first coaching discussion, all you need to do is ask for a referral.

If you ask "Do you know anybody who could?" etc the answer is likely to be, "No I don't, because you asked a closed question.

You may feel more comfortable by introducing a pre amble to your question. Don't be afraid to say "I obtain nearly all of my business by referral or word of mouth so, who else do you know who would benefit from meeting with me to discuss?" (Then your offering). Based on the fact that everyone knows someone and you have asked an open question, your chances of getting a referral have just gone up.

You can even ask someone for a referral who you have had a business meeting with and they decide it's not for them. You simply ask the same question as above.

It can't be that simple. Well I'm afraid it is. The only person stopping you from doing this is? Yes, you have got it again. It's Fred. But you know how to deal with him now don't you, so just ask the question anyway.

There are many other ways of getting business;

Direct mail

Yellow pages

Web sites

Leaflet distribution

And so on. Of course you can run some of these generic methods if you choose to. However, I am concentrating on the ones that will give you direct contact and exposure to your potential clients. They are no cost or low cost to you so your acquisition costs are minimal.

To summarise the 5 key areas

300 is your goal

Networking

Public speaking

Strategic alliances

Referrals

On top of which, you have just spent time and invested income in looking great.It would be a shame to keep that to yourself!

Your public awaits...

Chapter 4
So, why does my telephone weigh a ton?

The mind is like a parachute. It functions best when it is open. Ensure your mind is open when you read this and decide where you want to land. Which is, right in front of the person you want to see?

Now, picking up your telephone might not seem so tough as a telephone weighs just a few ounces. However for some it can be measured in tonnes, due to the fear that using the telephone for calling into a business holds. None the less, you are now ready to make use of all of those great contacts you have worked so hard to get. The result has to be worth the effort expended, by you. This is about reaping your 'sweat equity' Sweat equity is the amount of effort and energy you have generated and expended to get you to this stage in building a successful business.

I know there are hundreds of books, audio and DVDs on;

How to make an appointment.

How to overcome objections on the phone.

How to get past the "gatekeeper" (these people used to be called a secretary or P.A.)

How to use influence to get an appointment

67

I reviewed a CD recently on 'cold calling' and the list of things you have to do to get the appointment included;

"Getting to yes"

"Objection handling"

"Why objections are buying signals in disguise"

"Turning a no to a yes"

"The power of silence"

And so on...

Ok, ok stop right there. No wonder some people are scared of this! Let's look at this simply and make things happen in a nice, easy way. As coaches, you are all used to generating options and gaining a commitment to action. (The Options and Willingness in the GROW model).If you can do this you can breeze this part of gaining business.

"Heresy" I hear all the sales trainers cry. "It's hard to do. You have to understand the techniques, you need us to show you all how to be successful and what's more, salespeople don't like cold calling."

Ok then. How about this?

If you don't like cold calling then don't do any. That was easy wasn't it? After all, what is the point of gaining your freedom and running your own business if you end up doing something you don't like? If you are, then I suggest you need a coach. (Give me a call!!)

On the other hand, if this is part of your strategy, you still do not need to cold call. Make sure every telephone call you make is positive i.e. you just believe and expect that every person you call up wants to hear what you have to say and therefore it is not a cold call.

This is really easy to do. Treat every call as warm and that will make you feel a whole lot better about it.

The last time I made a cold call was in the late 70s and you know what? I don't think I will make one again.

Please make sure the end result of your call is not an appointment. Never ever make an appointment. I make those to see my dentist or doctor. Fix a business meeting instead. It sounds more important and it is more important. Buyers of your services will get dozens of calls from people wanting an appointment, so here is your chance to be just that little bit different again.

The business meeting is booked with those contacts you haven't yet met, all the other contacts you have generated at seminars, presentations, networking events etc. you have met. So all these calls are simply follow up calls to re-acquaint yourself with the person and to get a mutually convenient time in both of your diaries. It's important to stress the mutual part because, it tells the contact that your time is just as valuable as their time and if you can see someone at the drop of a hat it doesn't say much for your business, (or perhaps it does?)

Key message

Your time is just as valuable as the person you want to meet. So you are not about to waste their time or, for that matter, yours.

Here are some well worn phrases used by salespeople that tend to lead nowhere,

"I'm in the area" – That would make me feel really special as a buyer. So, you are not putting yourself out for me are you?

"I was just wondering if" – What on earth does a wondering coach look like?

"Can I pop in to see you" – Well if you like, but don't expect me to be here.

"For a chat about" – A chat? I haven't got time for a chat.

If, when you arrive, the appointment has cancelled and the contact has gone fishing don't be surprised. You were in the area anyway so it's not an inconvenience is it now?

The fact you have travelled for over an hour to get there is totally irrelevant, because you told the contact you were in the area, wanted a chat and only wanted to pop in anyway. Salespeople use these phrases because they are so easy to say. Why? Because they expect nothing of the person they are calling, and are trying to make it all sound convenient. It's an easy way to start a conversation and it places zero pressure on the contact and of course you.

Key Message
Make the person you want to see feel special and ensure they know you are travelling just to see them.

The very first thing to do, if you are making a proactive call is, leave the phone on the hook, until you are ready and prepared to talk. This does not mean putting it off. (Remember we decided to make this easy and simple to do).

Do some very simple research first;

If your contact has a web site have a look at it and find out about their business,

Know exactly where they are,

Perhaps they have won an award,

Or are celebrating a business anniversary,

Perhaps they have just moved offices and have new premises.

All this sort of information will put you in a good frame of mind before you call. You may get a chance to use it. If not then save it until your meeting.

Now get yourself ready.

Decide how long you will be doing this activity and stick to it.

You may decide on an amount of time you wish to allocate.

Or number of calls you will make.

Or a number of business meetings you want to book.

Decide which days you will allocate to this activity to give yourself the best chance and to ensure you have a variety of activity. This shouldn't be a slog, or something you have to beat. If it becomes either of these things then the contact will be able to tell from your tone of voice and your phrasing.

Whatever you choose to do, it's important to have a goal.

Make sure you have your diary to hand.

Know the dates you want to book the business meeting for.

Does your pen work? The number of people who find they don't have something to write with in a meeting would amaze you.

Finally and importantly, you really need to have a word with Fred. It is vital that you are in the most positive frame of mind possible. If you are not, the voice gives it away, hesitant, apologetic, mumbling, umming and ahhing all over the place, err, hum see what I mean? These are known as fill words. If you want to get rid of these fill words practice talking to people and consciously remove them from your conversation and notice the experience.

Here's a way to get your self into a powerful state. Recall a time when you were at your most:

Positive,

Powerful,

Unstoppable,

Determined,

Enthusiastic,

Successful

Really bring that time back to life today, here now, then consider the goal you are about to fulfil. I bet you set about making those business meetings with a different mindset and a flourish.

What's your goal?

It isn't to sell your service over the phone that's for sure. Nor is it to inform the contact about the benefits of coaching or your speciality. The purpose of the call has one objective and one only.

To book a business meeting.

If the person is out or in a meeting or unavailable then talk to the secretary or PA in a way that enables them to remember you.

You should aim to be on the phone for no longer than about 2 to 3 minutes. That's all it takes to arrange a business meeting. Any longer, and you are doing something else.

Remember, the longer you talk the more chance the contact has to say no. The more information you give the less reasons there are for the person to see you -e.g.

"So now I have informed you of the psychological roots of coaching and discussed how it works and told you the cost, can I book that business meeting?"

"No thanks. You have given me everything I need. Goodbye. Thanks for calling."

All that's left is a dial tone...

So be concise

The Lords Prayer has 67 words

The constitution of The United States of America has 453 words

The EEC document on the importation of aubergines has 15,553 words

Source unknown

Instead, adopt a different approach. When asked a question on content or price or what coaching is all about, acknowledge the question.

"I'm glad you asked me that. That's why I want to book a meeting with you to discuss that point and any others that you may want to raise. Do you have your diary to hand?"

If the answer is yes then just go ahead and book the mutually convenient date and time.

If the answer is no, then simply say you will hang on, or ask who books the diary. Ask to be put through and speak to them to book the meeting.

That's it for stage1. Very simple isn't it?

I heard that response from here!

Yes it is that simple. No I am not mad, and yes, it does work.

What follows is a testimonial from a person who really hated cold calling and found it difficult to get those appointments. We worked together for just 2 hours on the things you have been reading. Nothing more. The results? Well, see for yourself.

Senior Account Manager-Telecommunications

"Amazing results Neil. The frustrating thing is I now have more clients wanting to see me than space in my diary. This week I got the largest contract to date, a direct result of the coaching approach."

But what if it doesn't go like that? The one I described, is an easy one to deal with. However was it easy prior to reading this or after?

Of course you may get,

"I'm not interested."

"It's too expensive."

"It's not for me."

"I'm too busy."

And so on and so forth...

The simple way to deal with this is probably not the text book approach. I don't see objections as a buying signal, or as one step nearer to yes. If someone raises a block the chances are they don't agree or don't understand, so recognise it for what it is. It's simply a block to progress.

The process to follow is very simple; if the person raises a block or objection agree with them. That's novel isn't it?

Just say, "I can understand why you might think that, some of my best customers thought that at first until we had talked it through. I would like to do just that. Do you have your diary to hand to arrange a business meeting?" And yes we are back to the same place as the scenario above.

Perhaps though, the timing is not right for them to see you. The only way to find out is ask, so ask. Then agree to call the person back at that time or better still, forward book the meeting. Always look for the simple uncomplicated way of achieving what you want.

You can make this as difficult as you like. I suppose I should write some really complex stuff on gatekeepers as well. So if the secretary says, "the person is not in. Can I help?" say "yes you can. When is a good time to call?" or "I know diaries are the difficult bit to co ordinate and I know too well how salespeople (this differentiates you) want time. However I want to book this business meeting. What options does X have?"

Again we are back to the same place as above. Always aim to get the diaries together and book that business meeting.

Key Message
Always aim to get alongside the person who manages the diaries. They may not make decisions to buy but they are huge influencers and can make your life so much easier or much more difficult. The choice is yours.

I recall working with a team of people whose job it was to book appointments for the sales force. They were having problems getting the appointments and the sales force was consistently on their back. Morale was pretty low. We worked for half a day on their self confidence and spent a small amount of time on the above phrases. They then went on the phones. In 2 hours they arranged more meetings than they had arranged in the previous month. They were absolutely amazed with themselves. Even better, it was a Friday afternoon, but we all know you can't book appointments on a Friday afternoon. You are right, you can't, but you can make business meetings if you have the right frame of mind.

Key Message
If a buyer does not meet people who call they are not doing their job. A buyer is paid to buy.

Imagine a buyer's year end appraisal...

Buyer; "Well boss, lots of people tried to see me but I didn't see anybody new or purchase anything new all year."

Boss; "Hmm, let's talk about that shall we?"

Key Message
Imagine all the tasks you have to do and these tasks as frogs. The message is simple. If you are going to eat a frog eat the ugliest one first.
Brian Tracey

How about email? It's the 21st Century

You can of course use email to get your message directly into your contacts inbox, along with hundreds of other emails they have to read. Bear in mind ,if this is the first contact from you they won't know you at all, and may consider it SPAM. So if you are going to use this method think of an unusual title, something that gains the interest and then use a different approach in the text.

A very simple and direct way is this,

> "I want to do business with you. I would be grateful if you would let me know what needs to happen to enable us to meet. As I am a coach I imagine you would expect me to get right to the point."

> Regards

> xxxxx

I know this is effective because I have used this approach and so does a colleague of mine who reminded me of this simple approach. This is also a great follow up email once you have made contact, but cannot seem to make progress.

I recall looking to gain a business meeting with a particular organisation. Having used the phone and adopting all the key principals. I had spoken to the key contact but could not fix the meeting. So I sent the following email;

Title - Help

Text – I have tried everything but can't get you. What do you recommend I do next?

I received a phone call. The contact was laughing and said,

"What a refreshing approach. I have been so busy but your note made me laugh. When can we meet?"

The rest was easy.

What about letters and direct mail?

You have a letter template in this book, and of course you can use a direct mail approach. Look for something different. Instead of a letter what about a postcard? Or an invite, or a traditional 3 gatefold leaflet. As long as you keep it concise include the WIIFM, (what's in it for me?), why should I respond, what are the benefits to me and where is the call to action? Then follow them up by telephone. You will get a better response; you are in control and managing the client.

"Come on. Its just Junk mail."

Well yes. It can be to some, but for the person who responds it is targeted mail. There are people who buy a magazine and shake it so the leaflets fall out. However, some people just don't do that. There are two main types of direct mail. Firstly, the sort that goes out to homes and in personal purchase publications. The decision to respond is yours and mine. We don't need to consider anything else if the insert is of interest to us.

The second is the type that goes into organisations to a named person. The decision here is very different. Assuming the person reads it, the questions are, is this of interest? Do we do this already? Have I got enough information to respond? What are the implications for the current methods of developing people? Can I be bothered? And so on.

So ensure you choose your data list carefully. This means go back to your 300 contact list or your focused marketing model. Make sure you hit all the points you want to get across and remember, be concise.

Just stop and think about it for a moment. Direct mail must work otherwise why would organisations spend millions on it?

Perhaps because;

They can

They have a budget to cover the costs

They know the 1% return they will get and subsequent revenue will cover the cost of the exercise

They know the acquisition costs

They have a data base

It works, otherwise they would not do it

The questions for you are;

Do you have the above resources (financial and human) to carry this out effectively?

Do you have the expertise to do it and to continue to mail people until they surrender? Especially if you are just starting out.

Do you want the investment it will take up front?

The answers you come up with will tell you if this is for you.

Of course, you will still need to pick up the phone when you get a response.

Are you back to where we started on this? The telephone.

I will leave you answer that one!

Chapter 5
Preparing for the business meeting

Before you go to any meeting, there are three key things you need to do to ensure you are confident and ready. In no particular order they are;

1. Prepare – your meeting structure
2. Prepare – your documentation, facts and evidence and make sure they are to hand
3. Prepare – yourself, be in a positive state, your most powerful self

Preparing your meeting structure

Most business meetings follow a clear structure with you in control; there are many sales models used in the market place. For example Huthwaites SPIN (Situation, Problem, Implications, Need and Pay Off) model is probably the best known. Imagine a meeting starting with a broad opening with free discussion taking place, narrowing down to a specific point at the end, like an inverted triangle.

A Sales Model.

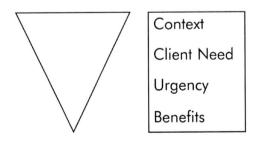

Context

Client Need

Urgency

Benefits

In this model each section is defined quite clearly, so think about it as a structured conversation that enables you to gather all the information you need as you look to achieve specific things from your client.

Context – this is about their organisation.

What do they do?
What is its structure?
How many staff do they have?
Who are the people who really make a difference?
And so on.

This is where your coaching skills come in, to get the contact to talk freely; it will be a novel experience for them as most salespeople will talk about themselves and their product.

The best way to do this is to stay with your open questioning skills. Just to remind you of these, they are questions that the contact cannot answer "yes" or "no" to. They start with;

Who
What
When
Where
How

There is of course **why,** but I am going to suggest you don't use why. Why is that? It's because after why comes the answer **because,** which is a justification of an action. When asked why most people revert back to childhood, where the word why is used more often than any other questioning word, e.g.

Why are you late?
Why haven't you cleaned your room?
Why did you do that?
Why did you break that glass?

So in short the question that begins with **"why"** will get you an answer that is a justification of a person's actions. We are not looking to hear a justification. We want to hear ideas and solid reasoning. At this stage of the conversation it may well be an unformed thought which is perfectly ok as this unformed thought will be developed into action a little later in the conversation. The word **"why"** also narrows down a person's thinking, whereas **"what"** opens up the mind to possibilities, or the art of the possible.

Client Need

This section of the conversation is simply about taking the key pieces of information from the background and establishing the contact's needs. I want to continue with the theme of keeping it simple and easy. To find a need, just ask the contact what their need is.Now that's not so hard is it?

A couple of example questions could be:

"What was it that made you agree to see me?"

If the contact says, *"Because you called me."*

Your reply is still the same with a reframe question.

"I'm sure you are busy and you don't meet with people for the fun of it, so what was it I said that made you agree to the meeting?"

All you do then is listen to the answer.

The contact will then quite happily tell you what they are looking for, their area of interest and why they will buy what you have to offer.

Easy isn't it? By the way, it works.

Urgency

In this part of the conversation your goal is to ask the contact questions that make the situation alive and very real. The contact is asked to think about the worst case scenario if they don't take coaching on board. A couple of sample question may be;

"What will happen if you don't develop your key staff members?"

"What do you think will happen if you make the organisational changes you have talked about and don't put the appropriate support in place?"

"Earlier you expressed a need to improve communication in your top team. What will the results be if you don't achieve this?"

Get the picture? Good; you are well on the way now.

Benefits

This is the final step. You summarise what has been agreed and simply match what you have to offer, in a way that meets the contacts needs.

That is all there is to it. I am sure you do this, can't you?

A different approach for coaches

This is all well and good and the model shown previously will work for you. However, you are a coach and you already have the relevant know how and use the GROW model in all your coaching interventions. So how about this as a thought? Rather than selling your services, you create an environment where you allow the contact to buy from you. Rather than lean towards the contact you use your coaching skills to encourage the buyer to lean towards you.

You can do this by simply adding a T to the GROW model making it TGROW, just like the inverted triangle described earlier. (Graham Alexander)

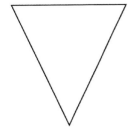

Topic - what are we here to talk about?

Goal – what are you looking to achieve?

Reality – what is the current situation?

Options – what could you do about it?

Willingness – how committed are you to taking this action?

You got it! Yes, it's a sales model and it's the same as the TGROW coaching model. How quickly did you spot it?

My conclusion is simple. If you can coach, you can sell.

It's that easy. You coach someone to buy from you.

I will repeat it. You coach someone to buy from you.

I really want you to know and understand this; get it into your thinking. Once it is firmly in place you will be amazed at just how well your initial business meeting flow.

Enter Fred! "I can see how this can work but, (yes it's that word again) how about this closing the deal business? I mean I have read so much about how businesses want 'good closers' and I don't think I am one of those."

Ok, if that's how you think then don't aim to be a good closer, aim to achieve securing the business.

I am sure that the methods of closing a deal are well known and you may have read about them all, so let's deal with this very simple area of the business meeting.

There are many types of closing remarks made and taught by sales trainers, I know this because I made them once upon a time. They can be effective for cold call salespeople. However, my belief is they are outdated and in any case most people who are in the business of dealing with salespeople know them off by heart.

They are;

The alternative close

"When would you like the contract to start? This month or next?"

"When is convenient for you? Thursday at 2-oopm or Friday at 11-ooam?"

This is pretty good when fixing your diary arrangements. However perhaps it's better to say,

"What dates look good for you in the next week?" – wait for the answer.

Then all you need to do is agree with the contact, providing you are also free. In this way you are simply matching diaries rather than pushing a meeting.

It works.

The assumptive close

Rather like the one I have just outlined.

"So, I will go ahead and draw up the contract then."

The direct close

"When do you want to start the contract?"

The reverse question close

"Does this come in blue?"

"If it does, how many do you want?"

So in your case, as a coach, you hear the question come across the table;

"Will you be carrying out 6 coaching sessions then?"

"If I am, will you go ahead?"

Or;

"Do you want me to carry out 6 sessions?"

Personally I don't like this at all. It's pushy and not very sophisticated.

There are more of these 'closes' around. However as I don't tend to use them I don't particularly want to recall them. Much better to simply go with the previous idea of coaching the contact to agree to do business with you and commit them to action using the willingness section of the TGROW framework.

As coaches' you already know how to do this don't you?

Chapter 6
The business meeting

The moment you have been working and waiting for!

- Your contacts have been built.
- Letters have been sent to potential clients.
- Telephone calls have been made.
- Your initial networking has been done, (although this is an ongoing process and never stops).
- You may have presented at an event or many events.
- You look like you mean business. Your first impression is spot on and very professional.
- Fred has had a good talking to and is in his rightful place.

You are faced with a simple choice right now,

You can either,

1) Listen to Fred who will be yelling at you, telling you all the things you don't want to hear and reminding you just how you failed at the egg and spoon race when you were seven, so you are sure to be;

Nervous – well that's ok.The very best people are always, yes always, a little nervous before a meeting. It keeps you sharp and on top form. If you are not nervous then you are either not alive to the possibilities and the situation or so blasé that you couldn't care less about the outcome.

Worried that you will mess it up – You won't.

You will forget a key point – You may well but that's ok.Only you will know and in any event you can always cover it later in the conversation or if it's that important and you happen not to recall it until after you have left, you can either telephone or send an email or both.

They won't want you – Yes they will.

They will ask you something you can't answer – You can answer all they need to know. If you can't answer something be honest and tell them you will find out and get back to them. That's perfectly acceptable. The only time it isn't acceptable is; if you promise to do this, forget to keep your promise and don't follow this through.

You will dry up – No chance. You are a coach. If you do feel lost, do what you have been trained to do. Summarise and ask a question. You are good at that. This will bring you back on track.

I won't know what questions to ask – Yes you will. You will ask the first question which is likely to be along the lines of;

"Tell me what's on your mind today," or

"Tell me what's on the table today. What is your thinking?"

And the rest will just flow as you relax into TGROW.

And so on and so forth.

Or you can choose to;

2) Tell Fred to shut up, be quiet and feed me something positive to enable me to perform at my best then just get on with the business of gaining business.

Fantastic. You decided on option two. Congratulations you are getting the hang of this. You are now ready to move onto the next stage.

Just as in coaching, the contact does all the talking. You just listen and prompt. Remember the old adage. You have two ears and one mouth. Use them in the same proportion!

Before you do anything at all, the first thing to establish is what the contact wants to get out of the meeting. Ask them what a successful outcome would be for them and what you need to leave them knowing. Just as in your coaching, you ensure you have set an end goal before you start, to enable you to focus both your efforts and the contact's in the right direction. You are now using the G in GROW. A great question to use is this;

"What do you want to have by the end of our meeting today?"

You also do not and probably need not launch into endless spiel about what coaching is, how it has developed and just how powerful it is. Time enough for that later in the meeting. The contact will ask you about this when they are ready to listen to what you have to say. Of course it may be they don't know what coaching is fully, or have it mixed up with other forms of developing people so perhaps you can help them out a little by simply giving the contact a snippet. The question is what snippet will you give? Full marks if you have decided to use your elevator speech at this point; it has all the key components you are likely to need, doesn't it?

If you need something a little more precise, here is an insight into the intention behind the five other common misconceptions about coaching. I think I need to make the point that this is in layperson's terms. I say this because I know some counsellors and therapists will have a much more detailed definition of their speciality. I have discussed this with many professionals in these areas and the debate has gone on and no doubt could go on for hours so, please accept the intent and let's move on. I am neither a trained counsellor nor therapist. I don't profess to have the skills to do this, I do have the skills to coach and if you have come this far then the chances are you do too.

Mentor - the intention is to guide
Trainer – the intention is to teach
Consultant – the intention is to recommend
Counsellor – the intention is to talk through
Therapist – the intention is to heal

This is of course, where many of the rogue coaches can blur the lines between the different disciplines (all requiring specialist training and skills) causing confusion and sometimes upset. No wonder the buying public and businesses are confused.

I think you will find the above intentions will help you in clarifying what coaching is and isn't. CECO clearly define coaching as a one-to-one, or one-to-team, goal centric, forward looking and forward moving process. The past has no relationship with the future unless the client allows this to become part of their particular issue. After all there is no point in rehearsing the past. We can't change it, so let's move on.

So here you are, using your coaching skills to enable the contact to buy your services, all you need to do when this point is reached is simply agree with the contact. It is that simple.

"Hang on just a minute; it can't be that easy, what about all the smoke and mirrors?"

There isn't any. Just plant this firmly in your head and go for it. After all, nothing happens unless someone sells something. Of course, I can take a couple more chapters to really complicate it for you if that's what you want. You can read the thousands of books that have been written on the subject of selling and really get yourself confused. However I suspect all that will happen is you will start to believe you can't do this and I certainly don't want that to happen and neither do you. Remember this is about coaching. It is not about technique based selling!

I am right, aren't I?

Key message

Let the contact talk, they will tell you all you need to know.

Handling Objections

I can almost sense that you want to know what to do if the contact raises objections. Maybe the first thing we need to look at is the definition of an objection. Please do not confuse a question, which is simply something the contact will ask to gain clarity, with an objection. These questions should not be seen as hurdles but are to be welcomed as it shows interest and engagement from the contact. Personally I love it when this happens as I feel that I am on the way when I am answering questions. Why? Not only because it shows interest, but also because I am on home ground, talking about what I know best. That's right. We are having a two way discussion to look at how we both can achieve the objective of getting coaching into the organisation.

An objection, on the other hand, is something the contact doesn't like. It's not a buying signal as some books would have us believe. It's an objection. I believe we need to be clear about this.

So, to begin I want to refer you back to objection handling, in the chapter on using the telephone. Most salespeople create their own objections so, don't create any!

For example, imagine you are selling briefcases and you say to a buyer;

"Here is a beautiful Italian calf leather briefcase; it comes in exclusive black, no structure to the case so it is really soft with a combination lock and brass fittings"

Just how many opportunities have you created in this simple statement to give the contact the chance to raise an objection and say. *"No thanks just looking."*

I think your statement has created five opportunities for an objection to be raised, they are;

- Calf
- Black
- Structure
- Brass
- Combination

In addition to the five objections or ways out of purchasing your product the statement only deals with the features of the case. There is nothing that gives the buyer the WIIFM factor, (what's in it for me, i.e. the benefits).

How can this be turned around, to sell the same product without creating these opportunities for the buyer to say no and therefore generate a different result? It is easy to do simply by using your questioning skills.

You ask *"What do you look for in a briefcase?"*

The buyer will then tell you what they ideally want.

Then you simply need to show the buyer how your case meets their ideal, i.e.

"When we designed this exclusive case we produced something for individuals who want quality in a product. This case has all the exclusivity that business people want when purchasing a quality product. Have a look at it, what do you think?"

Then shut up and wait for a response. We have already looked at how you deal with this response, so deal with it.

The way you may create your own objections to coaching are, if you are;

Hesitant about your fees. This gets a price objection.

Unclear about the results that the contact can expect. This raises a "what's in it for me?" objection.

Hesitating about your experience or training. This could raise a credibility objection.

Woolly on who else you have coached. This could say "I'm so new I'm practicing on you."

You coached people whilst you were training and gaining an accreditation, so ask them for a testimonial. If you don't have any then be honest with the contact. But please remember all the business and life experience you have, the training you have taken and the investment you have made in your chosen profession.

This counts for a lot and must not be overlooked.

Here are a few objections that may be raised;

"It's too expensive" – You can deal with this as the fee structure is something you own, and of course you have a choice whether to negotiate your fees or to walk away. If the contact is serious about your fee structure and their budgets are firmly set and they are not just looking to negotiate a better deal with you. Again you are in a position to make a positive choice about what you do next.

"It's not for us" – You can deal with this by asking, "What is it about coaching that is putting you off our services?"

Ask the question, wait for the response and answer it in a confident and relaxed manner as if it's something that you have answered many times before.

"We already use a coach" – You can deal with this. Be curious and find out what it was that encouraged the contact to see you in the first place? It's not as if the contact didn't know they had a coach, therefore there is a reason. Find out what it is simply by asking the question.

Or, go head to head with the other coach and agree to be put to the test. Gain agreement to coach a couple of individuals and just see how investment in your training and skills show a difference between your coaching and the existing coach, who of course may be a mentor, trainer or something else.

"Our people won't want to do this" – You can deal with this quite easily.

> How does the contact know this for sure?
> Do they know what coaching is?
> Do they know how it can help them?
> And so on.

Having looked at this area I am sure you will see just how simple it is to hold a discussion with another person. Potentially you are both there for the same reason, so don't be afraid of it or anxious. An objection may never crop up and if it doesn't, won't you feel cheated if you have worried about this area for days and days and have then not enjoyed the discussion?

It reminds me of buying something from a shop; the goods are faulty or have fallen apart in some way. We rehearse just what we will say to the shop manager, even to the point of quoting the Sale of Goods Act. We get all fired up walk into the shop utter those first carefully rehearsed words and the manager says,

"You are quite right I will change them immediately"

Hang on! You are not supposed to say that. I haven't given you my best shot yet and I rehearsed it for days! Don't we feel deflated? And what about all of that precious energy we have wasted on a non event?

Deal with whatever comes up at the time. You have the skill. Just use it!

The final area to consider is probably the single biggest fear of all, without any grounds, I might add. The fear of rejection. Someone might just say "No" and mean it. This is a fact of life. I am sure you have said no to things, or decided against doing business with someone. Just what did you reject? The product? Or did you make it personal and reject the person? We have already discovered that people buy people and the provider's actions and appearance can be a big turn off. However, as you have this right then the contact is not rejecting you, so there is no need to feel bad for too long.

Of course, you are going to be disappointed that the business did not come your way, so call the contact, thank them for their time and ask for feedback on the reasons behind the decision. In this way you learn what worked and what didn't, enabling you to be so much better the next time. It may also get the buyer thinking. "This person really cares about how they do business and took the time to call me. Perhaps I was wrong about them" and ask you to call in again. Or, they remember you when an assignment comes up. Disappointment aside, this is a learning experience, and as a coach you welcome feedback, don't you?

Concluding the meeting

As the meeting draws to a close, continue to use your coaching skills and ask the contact to summarise the conversation. This will let you know that they have taken in all the key points that have been made, by them and by you.

1. Ask the contact for their commitment to the next step, in coaching terms the W in GROW- willingness.

2. Ask the contact what happens next.

3. If they are not the final decision maker and you cannot get to see this person ask your contact what recommendation they will make.

4. Find out when the contact will be making a decision; make a note of the date.

5. Find out when is a good day to make a follow up call. Make a note of it. Please don't say,

   "I will call in a couple of weeks" What is so special about two weeks? So many people use this and frankly I just don't get that at all.

6. Always call before the decision day; you never know if anything has changed or if the contact needs any more information to make the decision. It's no good calling after the decision has been made. You cannot influence this at all; it's in the past and probably a done deal.

7. Finally, as you prepare to leave, let the contact know how much you enjoyed the discussion, thank them and tell them you will call on the agreed date.

8. Most importantly, shut up and leave. I have seen many people, who, having just had a wonderful dis-

cussion leading up to the decision point, and then carry on talking, out of context and begin to create doubt or raise questions in the contact's mind and possibly raise objections. Ouch! They leave with less than they went in with.

Key Message
Remember exactly why you are there; know when you have concluded the meeting, cut the small talk and leave.

Your product and its fee structure

So in a service industry where you are not selling a tangible, just what is your basic product?

What are you allowing the contact to buy from you?

How much should you charge?

I have asked this question to hundreds of coaches on CECO's open coaching programme and I keep getting the same answers which tend to be:

    My expertise
    Myself
    Goal achievement
    Confidentiality
    Behavioural change
    Increased performance
    Personal achievement
    Peace of mind
    The last one is the classic in most books on selling;

we sell peace of mind, (POM).
And so on and so forth.

All the above answers are potentially correct and at some stage of the meeting these points and needs, along with your skills, will play a part in agreeing a contract.

How about a different angle that will help you to be really clear about what you 'sell'? A very simple statement. Are you ready?

You are selling your time; the basic building block of your services is your time. Once you have this firmly in place then structuring and pricing your service is so much easier.

For example, let's assume you decide that a coaching day is six hours in length. I think this is about right; you will need time for a break, to clear your head and get ready for the next client. If you try to put too much into one day then you are likely to come undone. You will get tired and the chances are you will not be as fresh for the last person as you were for the first.

Let's also assume that in this example that you decide to set your fees at £1500-00 per 6 hour day.

This sets your hourly rate at £250-00

If the client has 6 people to coach and it is necessary to coach them for 2 hours each then you have 12 hours coaching.

2 days work
£3000-00
6 people at 1.5 hours = 9 hours = £2250-00
6 people for 1 hour = 6 hours = £1500-00

There are, of course, any number of combinations of the above and that is for you to decide when you are delivering a proposal or investment to the contact.

This method of structuring your fees enables the client to see and understand exactly how you have arrived at your contract price. It is also really transparent to the contact as well; this means, no surprises in terms of what is and isn't charged for in your fees. By adopting this approach you will also avoid any potential embarrassing moments when a client says "Can you just?" You have the option to say "yes" and do this as a gesture, or to say "yes it will take about 3 hours; you know the fees will be £750-00." The choice as always is yours. At least you will do this consciously rather than just giving away your time, your product. If you don't think of it this way then test it out. Go into the nearest car showroom and ask them if you can have their product for free. What answer do you imagine you might get?

Or in the local supermarket, nip in and fill your trolley with a weekly shop and say;

"I just wanted to try this out so I won't be paying for it. Is that OK?" they won't wear it and neither will the magistrate, because its called shoplifting!

Another tip that will stand you in good stead. If you are delivering a coaching programme to tutor people inside the organisation to coach, or you are asked to take a team coaching day, is to charge your day rate rather than the hours you are with the client. This will be appreciated and goes a long way towards generating goodwill and a great relationship with the contact.

You may also want to consider having a half day minimum fee charge. For example, if the contact wants you to coach just 2 people for 1 hour you may want to charge half a day i.e. 3 hours. On the other hand you may see this as a development opportunity by saying

"I am here for 2 hours; you have paid for 3 hours anyway, who else would you like me to coach whilst I am here?"

The reason for this is simple. You get an extra client which puts you inside the organisation a little more deeply, further cements the relationship with the organisation and the contact gets good value for their investment.

The Price is Right
So let's put this to the test – base all costs in this example at £1500-00 per day

Please note this is a real scenario

Your task is to price the brief set out below:

You are to present to the Board of 6 Directors, a proposal and costing based on a budget of 20k (which they have said is their maximum spend) for the successful delivery of a coaching programme which will be rolled out to 140 managers across the business, head office and branch network.

You are asked to enable the business to become self sufficient in the delivery of this programme as the aim is to introduce a coaching culture in the long term.

Your coaching audience and exposure will be 40 managers, including the board and 6 trainers.

You are 1 of 4 organisations presenting. You have the 3rd slot.

Your task is to determine;

How you will deliver the above brief for a 20k investment
What methods you will use during the presentation
The key message you must get across
How long it will take to deliver the complete programme
What your recommendations will be, given that this programme is business critical and supports a major investment in a Customer Relationship Management System (CRM) and new centralised call centre.

You have been introduced to the organisation via the General Sales Manager who has seen your profile. He is a great supporter of coaching. However he will not be at the presentation.

Your key contacts are the General Manager Learning and Development and his direct report the Management Development Coach.

Work out what you will deliver and how given the information you have.

You will be able to see what actually happened at the end of the book –No cheating now!

How much should you charge?

This is a personal choice. However, I can give you some thoughts to help you decide on your fees.

Now that you have decided to look at your product as time, the amount you charge in fees is directly related to your life energy. With that in mind, how much do you think your life's energy is worth, because that is what you will be exchanging for money?

Decide where you want to position yourself. What league do you want to play in, the 1st Division or the 2nd Division? Are you in the top flight designer stores or the bargain basement? This is an interesting dilemma; the shop front determines the cost of the goods. Therefore, the very same item in a top designer store can cost four times as much as the same item elsewhere. Make your choice and stick to it.

Your own self esteem and confidence will also play a big part in setting your fees. That little voice called Fred will come into play, telling you,

"You are never worth that much."

"No one will pay you as much as that."

And so on,

I hear of so many really good coaches charging fees at much less than they are truly worth, and the opposite is also true with very average coaches charging very high fees. In both cases, the coach will eventually be found wanting. The first scenario can be put right in the long run, the second not so easily, if at all. You may not even get the opportunity to do so.

The chances are that wherever you decide to pitch your fees, you will look back and wish that you had charged more for your services. Remember the client is receiving the benefits of all your personal experience, your investment in your training and accreditation, your continuous personal development and of course your life experience. You do not come to coaching as a blank sheet of paper.

This is all well and good, but where do you start? A survey carried out in 2001 by The Institute of Employment Studies stated that;

'Fees of around £2000-00 per day are not uncommon for an executive coach. This compares with the average of £975-00 per day for management consultancy.'

Whilst we can read figures like this and believe that this can be charged out as a matter of course, there is a fee that each market sector will stand. This simply reflects the type of business and sometimes location of the businesses you are targeting. You may also decide that your fees need to match your experience and the amount you are comfortable with. In other words, if you charge out at a high fee then you really need to be able to back that up with your coaching capabilities.

To put this in perspective and for your consideration only (this is not a recommendation) I know of one coach who has an annual contract with a public sector organisation which guarantees 100 days work p.a. which the coach charges out at £750-00 per day. This seems quite low when you look at the IES study, but this coach has secured an income of £75,000 p.a. immediately January 1st arrives, for 100 days work.

Put in those terms, how many coaches wouldn't take that contract when you are just starting out?

A note of caution I think. Please recall the chapter on coaches who are self styled gurus or the rogue coach. I have heard of these people talking about charging fees of any thing up to £10,000 per day. I ask myself, just how true is this? How much is simply a big ego, wishful thinking or a belief in their own PR?

Key Message
In terms of your fees, be true to yourself and my belief is you will not go far wrong.

Money is what we exchange our life energy for, so make it worthwhile.

Chapter 7
Following the Business Meeting

Well that's it. The piece of work you have probably been dreading is all over, and you have performed well. You have used your coaching skills to take you quite happily through the discussion and what's more, you didn't get a single objection that you could not handle. You answered questions and took your cues like a professional. That's one in the eye for Fred, eh?

You have done your very best and that is all anyone can ask; that you do the best you can with what you know. The time to give yourself a good talking to is when you do less than you are able to do and you know it.

The contact at this point may want something in writing, or they may not. Here is your next health warning;

If the contact doesn't want a proposal then don't offer to send them one!

It is oh so easy at this point for you to say;
  "I will confirm all this in writing."

Rather than simply ask;
  "When do you want the coaching to start?"

The moment you offer to do a proposal you have done a number of things. The positive is that you have confirmed the conversation and all the information that the contact needs.

But you have also;

Just extended the decision making time.

Given the contact a great chance to find a reason not to do the coaching.

Lost the urgency that has just been created in a mutual discussion.

Given the contact a chance to think of more questions to ask, (probably unnecessary questions at that).

Created the potential for others in the organisation to be involved in the decision.

Given the contact time to meet with another coaching provider to seek a competitive cost or pursue a different agenda with the need you have just created.

Generated more work for yourself in having to capture the entire conversation on a few pages and deciding which points are relevant.

Key message
If the contact doesn't want anything in writing to confirm the conversation. Do not offer it.

However, the contact and you will need something to outline what has been agreed and what you are about to do. Consider sending a simple letter of intent with your terms and conditions. You already know these and how you will structure your coaching from previous chapters.

Confirm when you will start.

Outline your fees. The client will already know the investment they are about to make as you have already discussed this.

Explain your cancellation charges, (i.e. if the client cancels your booked session at short notice) and of course thank them for the business and say how much you are looking forward to working with them. More of this a little later – see proposal template.

Let us assume though that a proposal is needed. There are a number of things to consider;

What will you put in it?

How will you structure it?

How much detail will you include?

How long is a proposal?

As with everything in this book for coaches; let's keep this simple to compile, easy to follow and most importantly, interesting to read. Think of your proposal in this way; you are putting in writing a summary of the key points that have already been discussed and agreed by the contact. As a coach this is another skill you already have. Coaches are used to giving feedback and summarising, so write your proposal in the first instance, as you would say it then edit it later. As with all great feedback and summaries, you won't add in anything that has not been said and agreed, unless you add in some research facts, case studies and your testimonials as evidence of your work. Remember the following phrase as it will serve you well and not just in proposal writing;

Feedback – evidence = opinion

In my view, an opinion is worth absolutely nothing unless the person who is on the receiving end of it places a value on that opinion. I am sure you would not want to put your professionalism and skill as a coach in the hands of another person's opinion, now would you? Ensure you always provide evidence.

To give you a starter for ten, I have included a proposal template that you can easily populate with the key points from your business meetings; add a dash of your own style and bingo! You have a very credible proposal. Of course, it's a catch all and you may want to edit some of the headings to suit your needs. If you are at that stage then congratulations. You are on the way to your proposal writing skills being enhanced.

Proposal template

The areas that I recommend that you cover in a full proposal are;

- A covering letter
- Introduction or Background
- Context
- Development needs
- Why coaching
- Proposed approach
- Recommendations
- Investment
- Next steps
- Appendices

The Covering Letter

This is simply acknowledging the fact that the meeting took place, between you and the contact. Here you use the contact's name and job title in full. That the meeting went well and that you felt it was good to meet with the contact to discuss the organisational needs against which this proposal is written.

That's about it. Any more and you are into the detail of the proposal itself.

Remember it's a covering letter, on your letterhead.

Introduction or Background

Here you repeat the issues that were raised in the meeting by the contact. The information will come from the opening of the meeting,(in coaching terms the Topic from TGROW.) You will also have information from the Reality stage so add in the relevant information. Please remember to use the following words;

"You stated..."
"We agreed..."
"You felt..."

This way you are aligning what has already been said in writing, and reminding the contact of the commitments that have already been made and placing the contact on your side.

Context
In this section it is vital that you have a context for your recommendations so you have to ensure you state all the key issues that the contact raised.

The examples below indicate some of the issues that you may have identified in your discussions.

This will identify the changes that the organisation has undergone or is undergoing.

- The culture of the organisation that is prevalent.

- The values and the vision of the organisation.

- Any previous investments that the organisation has made in supporting or initiating a change in direction or performance.

• Any other development initiatives that have been identified which need to be supported.

Development Needs

Where is the focus of the coaching to be?

Whether you are dealing with either individuals or teams or both.

Define any changes in behaviours that the organisation is looking for.

Identify if a performance issue needs addressing.

And so on,

You will have the bespoke items from the G in the TGROW coaching model.

Why Coaching ?

Identify why coaching is the solution as opposed to any other form of developing people.

You may also choose to show that coaching does not stop any other initiative that the organisation has underway. Whatever the organisation is currently doing, coaching will support it. In this way coaching is not fighting with any other person's initiative and therefore is not in competition with internal HR or L&D departments.

This is where you will show research and facts on the benefits of coaching; refer to your case studies and previous examples of work that has been carried out in this area.

The contact wants to know just one thing, WIIFM, what's in it for me.

Proposed Approach

What you will do, first to last.

What are the clear measures of success that have been agreed with the contact?

What implications are there for the participants?

Whether the coaching is face to face or telephone or a mixture of both.

What additional support methods you are including i.e. email.

When you will take your reviews of the coaching to show the success and participants reactions.

What feedback you will give to the organisation?

Recommendations

Identify how many coaching sessions each person will have.

How long each session will be in duration and how far apart.

Over what time scales.

The proposed outcomes.

Whether there will be any team coaching.

What orientation you will need to do if any.

What other information you will need prior to the coaching commencing.

What communication the contact will use to let the participants know the coaching is about to take place.

Investments
The cost of the programme

The number of days in total

Your daily and hourly fees if appropriate

Identify your expenses

- mileage

- hotels if required

- travel

- materials

VAT

Payment terms

Cancellation charges

Next steps

Your recommendations on what happens next.

What the contact has agreed to do.

The commitment the contact has already agreed to make.

(Which comes from the W in the TGROW model)

Identify that you will make a diary note to call the contact on the agreed date.

Appendices

1. case study
2. testimonials
3. your profile

Chapter 8
So you want to increase your turnover?

I guess this applies to you and hundreds of other coaches. However, whilst some people are in search of the Grail, you are reading this. Throughout my career I have worked with some brilliant managers and some who were not so good. How many of you have said. *"If I ever get to manage people, I will not treat them as this manager has treated me?"*

I learned a tremendous amount from the brilliant managers, but I also learned from the ones who were not so good.

There is a proven method of increasing your turnover, which I will illustrate by telling a story. This story shows the lessons I learned from the not so good managers.

Once upon a time (ok just go with it) there was a manager of a major blue chip organisation. This manager was all powerful and had some well worn phrases that he surely must have read in some tea leaves somewhere. He used these pearls of wisdom to motivate his staff to great efforts and achievements. They were;

1. If you see more people then you will sell more.

2. If you let the customer see your product price in the keenest light then you will sell even more.

3. The only thing that you need to do to get on in the world of business is to work hard, nothing else matters.

4. It's a wise man who knows his limitations.

5. You need to drive your support team as hard as you can. Don't spare the rod.

6. I will look at the call rate for sales visits each week and berate the salesman who does not achieve the magical rate, which I in my wisdom have decreed.

7. Whilst in the company car it is the duty of the salesman to ensure that each journey between two clients is the shortest, regardless of the quickest route. This cuts fuel costs.

These tactics never seemed to achieve what the manager wanted.

Ok let's get a little more serious now, I would not recommend that you adopt any of the above.

Let's take each statement in turn and analyse the effects of its implementation. A basic model would be useful to consider here.

Direction

Quantity   Quality

Imagine the triangle is equilateral, i.e. all the angles are equal and equal force is being placed at each corner. Let's look at the impact on this triangle when we apply the manager's pearls of wisdom.

Pearl of wisdom number 1. See more people

If pressure is exerted on the quantity end of the triangle, i.e. you pull the model left. That becomes your focus and the triangle loses its shape. You will also lose the quality of the customers you are seeing and you lose your direction. This is a result of the policy which is "see more people and you will sell more products." The translation is, "throw more mud at the wall and some will stick."

I guess this is true. However it assumes that you have enough mud to throw and that your database is infinite. You may of course just end up with a muddy wall. This is a hit and miss process with very little planning or strategy. It is a numbers game only. It will work for a short time and then it dries up.

The model now looks like this;

Direction

Quantity   Quality

What happens then if you exert pressure on the quality end of the triangle? i.e. you pull the model to the right This is about only seeing those clients who are seen as the big clients with the big budgets. In this strategy you are doing what many key account salespeople do, relying on hitting the one big client that saves the day. In reality, of course you are not seeing enough clients, your diary is pretty empty and again you have lost that key shape to your business.

Direction

Quantity　　　　　Quality

This strategy is called **"all your eggs in one basket"**, again not something I would recommend.

The penultimate part of the story is if you just work hard, in one simple stroke you could lose everything you are working for. Your ability to really strategise what you want and how to get it are dismissed in our manager's tale. You simply cannot afford to lose direction which, after all, in the chapter on building your client database you worked hard to find. In this diagram your business is flattening out as your energy is sucked out of you. You are potentially becoming a 'busy fool'

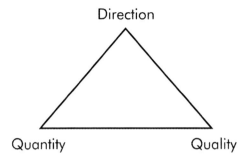

This strategy simply put is, anywhere, anyhow, any time, any place and because you don't know where you are going any road will take you there. Of course you are working hard giving you a false sense of productivity, except your books won't even begin to show any increase in turnover.

And finally;

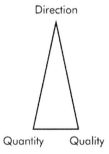

Blast off!

Enough said about this diagram, you have lost it all. You have spent a long time deciding on where you want to go. However, you have done little or nothing about it. This is called **NIPA** or non income producing activity.

So it's about balance, the 'right' quality, with the 'right' quantity within your chosen direction or market etc. I cannot define the word 'right' for you, however if you look back at your business planning model then you can determine this for yourself.

Pearl of wisdom number 2. Sell on price

This is about selling your services at any price. You have decided on your fee structure so stick to it. Of course you may choose to negotiate a little if the contract has some volume or you can really see the potential in the client. This is up to you but please don't fool yourself into thinking all price reductions are good for the client. One of my organisational contacts has a great phrase when looking at fees;

"Pay half pay twice"

A nice way of saying, *"you get what you pay for."*

Pearl of wisdom number 3. Work Hard

There I was digging this hole, a hole in the ground. Big and sort of round it was!

The trouble is, as we have discussed, if you are digging it in the wrong place then its all for nothing.

"Hard work is all that counts." He said.

"What about the minor details like, knowing where to dig for gold, plus your skill, talent ,creativity, innova-

tion and all those characteristics that make up a great coach that you have just spent time and energy building. Are they just mere details?" I yelled back.

Pearl of wisdom number 4. A wise man knows his limitations

I can only call this statement a heinous crime against another person's ambition. I spend a lot of my time helping my clients to expand their horizons. The limitations that they tend to have are those they place upon themselves. These limitations can be learned in childhood or from managers just like the one in our story.

Pearl of wisdom number 5. Berate the team who are helping you

Berate the person or team who is striving hard and doing the best they can to help you! Why on earth would anyone want to break this person's will and motivation? After all they are on your side. Isn't this a sure fire way to de-motivate them? Surely as a skilled coach you will use this skill to enable the person who is helping you to achieve more, and then keep a gentle hand on the tiller.

Sometimes you won't even notice that someone is trying to help you. The reasons can be numerous, however it could be that, when you have your nose to the grindstone, back against the wall, shoulder to the wheel, ear to the ground and your eye on the ball it's a bit tricky to see where you are going, don't you think?

Hello! Take a look up and see what is going on then recognise those people who want you to do well. Then thank them.

Pearl of wisdom number 6. The magic call rate

Let's cut to the chase here.

Beat up a salesperson because they haven't hit a magic number set by someone who doesn't have to do what you are about to do? The only person who can determine your call ratio is you. So please set this ratio as you would any goal. That is SMART. Don't be fooled into competing with someone else who tells you. That they see 30 contacts a week, or conversely they only need to meet with one. Yes of course, you need to see enough people but please don't forget the basic triangle shaped model shown earlier. Keep your attention on the three points of the model equal. The race is long and in the end the only person you are competing with is yourself.

Pearl of wisdom number 7. Take the shortest route

Cut fuel costs? Seems logical and it is a sensible thing to do. However it assumes the shortest route gives the best fuel economy. This isn't always the case.

These pearls of wisdom are taken from a true story. Its my story from a time when I was an employee under this manager, here are the facts.

Target call rate 22 visits per week

Actual call rate 20 visits per week

I was also the highest producing salesperson in the branch and region; I was the second highest producer in the country. I did not lose existing clients and in fact grew our penetration within them.

But, my call rate was 2 below the target. The result was, my call rate was increased to 27 per week. I had just had the "mud at the wall" technique delivered right on my desk. Behind my past results sat the triangle of quantity, quality and direction, I was guiding the person who was helping me rather than driving them hard and I gave some thought to expenses! So, no surprises that my productivity went through the floor. I went against everything I seemed to subconsciously know in order to meet the targets. I didn't have the time to manage my existing clients therefore I lost some of those. I also lost the additional business from the client penetration I was achieving through managing the client relationships. The weird thing was my manager seemed happy.

Why? I was hitting 27 calls per week. Funny old world isn't it?

Just pretend for a minute that you are my manager's boss, looking at this decline in a person's performance. What would you do?

Well, he was a reasonable man and asked some questions. I was asked to explain what had gone wrong and

I did so. Guess what? My triangle was restored, decisions reversed and my results picked up again.

The reason for the story? Simple really. It shows in real life (not theory) what can happen if you let your business get out of shape.

Key message
It's your business, your plan, your efforts and your structure. Why on earth would you let someone else determine how you run the business? Seek advice when you need it. However choose wisely whose advice you seek.

Remember advice is only a way of recycling the past, take the bits you need and discard the pieces you don't want.

If you aim to increase your turnover then I suggest you look at increasing your profitability at the same time.

There are many ways to do this and many books to tell you how. However I am going to continue the trend of keeping it simple and look at four key contributing ratios;

- What is your conversion rate from lead to qualified contact?
- What is your conversion rate from contact to business meeting?
- What is your conversion rate from meeting to contract?
- What is your average size of contract?

Database

You can impact these ratios through careful marketing, networking and lead generation. Qualify your contacts, gather information at the first meeting with them and ensure the quality you are looking for is there.

On the telephone

Note down what you say, what works and what doesn't. Also note down your mood, the time of day and the days you have the most success. In this way you can ensure you remove any bad habits that may intrude and maximise your natural abilities.

At the Business Meeting

Ensure you are prepared and that you are in "a good state." If not, then change your state by sitting upright (no slouching) smiling and really energising yourself. If you have set a positive anchor then fire it up. Again be aware of what you say and what scores with the contact. A positive anchor is when you can easily recall a time when you were in an enthusiastic, motivated, determined and successful state of mind. Then bring these anchors to the fore in the situation you are currently facing.

Contract Size

Please do not be afraid of recommending your solutions even if it sounds or feels expensive to you. It may not be to the client. Manage the account and build a great relationship with the organisation for repeat business and the additional opportunities that will come your way.

Then and only then, will you be happy ever after in your own story. There is one key difference between the story I told and yours. Why? Because you are not impacted by someone else's views on how to run your business. The only person you have to answer to is the person who looks back at you every morning from the mirror. In addition you don't have the manager to deal with. All you need to deal with is 'Fred' and you now know how to deal with him.

When you think about your business keep this phrase in mind. *"I don't want to be a busy fool. I do want to be busy and profitable."*

You know what? I wouldn't have it any other way would you?

Bill Shankley the legendary manager of Liverpool FC said to his players:

"Every time you touch the ball, make it the most important touch of your life."

The same is true every time you come into contact with a potential client.

Key Message
The difference between those who do and those who don't are those who do something about it.

Chapter 9
Structuring your coaching and setting up the relationships for success

Once you have achieved your aim of securing a contract and the coaching itself is about to begin (the bit you have been waiting for) the next thing to focus on is setting up the coaching and structuring the discussions. Spending a little time doing this properly will put you way ahead of other coaching organisations. The coach who had this contract and didn't do this simple piece of work has just discovered that they made an expensive mistake. An omission that the coach who lost out is unlikely to ever recover from with this particular organisation. As a professional coach you should always strive to achieve the very highest levels of building and sustaining professional organisational relationships.

The people who don't make it are those who do not invest in themselves, and to quote an earlier message, the difference between those who do and those who don't are those who do something about it. You have done something positive, invested in yourself and have started down the road to become a professional executive coach.

Once you have the contract, to ensure the coaching is a success and the results can be measured, you really need to work in a triangular relationship with the organisation.

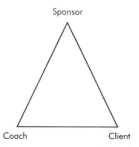

Sponsor

Coach   Client

Each client will have a sponsor. This is likely to be the client's line manager, although sometimes it can be the person who contracts the coaching. i.e. maybe H.R, L&D or the business sponsor. Prior to your first coaching session with the client it is absolutely vital that you discuss with the sponsor the key themes for your coaching. In this meeting you are looking to establish;

- What makes coaching the chosen method of developing the individual?
- What are the key measures of success? Which of course will be specific and measurable.
- What are the reasons for the coaching relationship?
- What is the current situation?
- How the outcomes will be measured?

In other words, it is just like any other coaching discussion. Well, actually, it is a coaching discussion.

The very next question to ask after you are both absolutely clear about why you are there is this;

"Have you had this discussion with the person I am about to coach?"

If the answer is "yes," then all is well and good. You will be meeting with the client and any management messages have been delivered openly to them.

If the answer is "no," then it is not recommended that you start the coaching and you simply encourage the sponsor to hold the discussion with the individual. The reason for this approach is very straightforward. As a coach you are not there to deliver a message to the individual that may come as a surprise. You are not there to deliver either good or bad news. It is much better if the line manager does this.

If you allow this to happen and go ahead with the coaching, you are just delaying the inevitable conversation that will take place at some point between the manager and the employee. If you deliver the feedback, then you may also be needlessly worrying the client by delivering the message second hand. It only takes a minor inflection in your voice and tone, in just the wrong place and you have nowhere to go. It is almost impossible to carry on the coaching as the client will want to know exactly what their manager has said and means. In short just let the sponsor/manager deliver the message. It is not your role to do so.

Key Message

I cannot stress this point enough. You are not there to deliver news to your client. Encourage the sponsor to have the same conversation with the client as they have just had with you. It is a manager's/sponsor's role to do this.

In this way all of the people involved in the client's development are fully aware of what is happening and why. You also know the key measures of success; these are the things that your intervention will be measured on. You are now able to align your coaching accordingly. Remember, this is a business arrangement and this is just one reason executive coaching differs from life coaching, in that there are more than two people involved in the outcomes.

Once the coaching sessions are completed along with the mid term and final reviews. The effectiveness of the coaching has been assessed by the client and the sponsor and the return on investment can be established (ROI).

Whoa there. What's all this about mid term and final reviews?

Ok. Let's say you have six coaching sessions with the client. You will ask for feedback from the client at the end of each session on how useful the coaching has been and you will measure the outcomes against the client's goals for the single session. Following the third session, you will hold a mid term review. In this review you will be seeking more specific feedback from the client; you may decide to design a review form with very specific questions to establish whether the coaching is on track and to find out exactly what he/she thinks about you as a coach. You can then either leave the form for the client to complete and return to you, or you may build it into the coaching session for the last 15 minutes or so.

This information is then shared with the sponsor. No, it is not breaking confidentiality because you are not asking for, or disclosing the client's issues or concerns. You are asking for their reaction to your coaching and you as a coach.

The final review, after session six is a combination of all six coaching sessions, to establish how the client feels about the progress they have made from their original start point and against their goal which was aligned to the business goals you agreed with the sponsor. It also shows the client just how far they have come in a relatively short space of time. You will also be reviewing the feedback against the measures of success. Once this review with the client is complete then you need to set up a meeting with the sponsor to discuss the outcomes.

You will of course be explaining all of this to the client at the outset of your coaching agreement with them. The client will know feedback is expected from them and that you will be discussing in general terms the progress being made with the sponsor. Again it is vital that there are no surprises here. In this way the client is fully aware that this is a business decision to involve a coach and that the organisation is making a significant investment in the individual in terms of money and time.

The coaching relationship is now set up for success. Unless...

What happens if you have 12 clients with three line managers in one organisation and HR have contracted the coaching?

The answer is just like all the other solutions in this book, keep it simple. If you stop and think about this for just a minute then you can see that all you need to do is replicate the process for a single client and simply scale it to meet the needs of a business sponsor and three line managers.

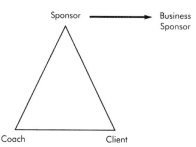

You are now working in a model that looks like this.
Your HR contact is now the business sponsor in this case and a separate discussion is held with this contact to establish the measures of success and context for the coaching. Along with the business or programme objectives. It is structured along the same lines as outlined previously. You will be establishing the business objectives and the outcomes HR are looking for, these could be anything from;

- Changing the organisational culture to a coaching culture
- Creating an atmosphere that encourages open and free communication
- Defining or refining organisational values
- Defining acceptable behaviours
- Supporting a change process
- Embedding a training initiative
- And so on,

There is one thing that I want to draw your attention to here; the above would not be acceptable by a great coach as measures. Why? Because they are too woolly. Some words can mean just about anything depending on who is reading them. Words like,

Coaching culture
Atmosphere
Acceptable
Supporting

These are not clearly defined and should you go along with these, do not be surprised if at the end of the coaching, the business sponsor says;
"That's not what we meant."

It's too late at this point and you will not be covered in glory.

The measures need to be clear and specific, in other words make sure they are SMART:

Specific
Measurable
Agreed
Realistic
Timebound

Some of you may be familiar with SMART and know that in some cases the A means achievable. In this case, to ensure the line managers involvement, I would suggest you go with Agreed. You could also argue that Realistic and Achievable can mean the same thing? I guess you need to decide!

You will be asking the HR contact to communicate the fact that coaching is about to take place to all the people involved. In this way, you will not arrive at your first meeting or make your initial phone call, cold.

Each manager will have a session with you and each individual who reports to that manager will be discussed in the way we have already looked at. The same questions are asked about each person and the manager is encouraged to communicate to them what they have communicated to you. So you have three sponsor meetings discussing four individuals at each meeting.

The mid term and final reviews take place in exactly the same way as before except you have twelve of each in three sets of four, one for each line manager. Finally, you have one overarching report for the business sponsor, in this case, your HR contact

At last, your coaching has been set up for success, there are no holes in your process or thinking, nothing can trip you up or stop you from achieving the business outcomes – unless of course, Fred pops in for a chat. After all you haven't heard from him in a while and he figures you are getting lonely.

The only things in your way now are your clients and you know how to deal with those, because you have taken the time to become trained and you know exactly what you are doing.

Chapter 10
Accelerating your business

How fantastic would it be if you could achieve more revenue through your fees by doing less work and putting in less effort?

This is a common mistake that many people, not just coaches; make when a business (your business) begins to grow, or when you have been running at 100mph for some time. All the great work that you have put in so far, as you have been following this book, suddenly starts to pay off. What happens next is predictable; the great work that you have done suddenly starts to ease off. By the way, this happens to employed sales forces and most people who are into revenue generation. There are two very clear scenarios that occur over and over again. I invite you to really stay with this chapter and to place yourself in the positions that I will describe. In this way you will be thinking along the lines that will serve you well and as a result you will be able to notice if you begin to fall into the habits that won't serve you well. In this way the key messages will come through to you loud and clear.

Scenario One
Effort versus Results

'I know from my own experiences that the initiatives we want to put in place are true and work for most people I work with, for most of the time.

They do work allowing for the odd freak, criminal or madman. To use them, however, to go beyond the understanding into action, requires, often, a degree of
courage (to go against convention)
trust (that people will behave as you expect) and considerable
patience (because the world turns slowly and people do not change their colours or behaviours overnight)'

**From "Inside Organisations"
Charles Handy**

When someone starts a new business venture how much effort would you expect them to put into it in the first 6 months?

The usual response is 100%. I often hear people say "I will give this 110%", which is of course absolute nonsense. As we only have 100% of ourselves to give. What I am about to tell you is true. I have seen it in both employed salespeople and in self employed people. The analysis graph proves to be correct for most situations for most of the time. As you are now about to be made aware of it, then it will not happen to you.

Effort vs. Results

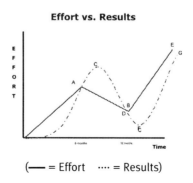

(——— = Effort   ···· = Results)

So the initial effort line on a graph for the first six months is likely to look like the bold line.

The results line however will take a much gentler curve before it meets the dotted effort line at point A.

The reason is due to a time lag between the effort or initial contacts and the results flowing through.

At point A however, when the two lines meet, the initial thought process is. "Hey I have made it! I am getting the results I need."

What happens to the effort line at this point?
It actually starts to reduce to point B as the feeling of "I have done it" kicks in and you ease off.

What happens to the result line?
It doesn't go down. It continues to go up to point C, because you are now reaping the rewards of your initial efforts in the 1st few months, which you can see from the low initial result curve.

The thought process now, is very dangerous.

"Wow! I really have cracked it. I am now putting in half the effort and getting twice the result."

So the effort line carries on down.

The result line now falls like a stone to point D; you have no residual effort to bale you out.

The thought process now is,

"Oh my goodness" (or words to that effect) *"I had better pump in some more effort."* This can only happen once you have re-motivated yourself. Do not despair. Your next action is your lifeline.

So in goes the extra effort and the effort line goes up very sharply to point E.

The result line however keeps going down to point F, because of the time lag again.

The thought process now is,

"I have lost it. Its all gone. I can't do this anymore. My initial success was pure luck."

No, it wasn't. Keep going and the result line will pick up again to point G.

You know what to do. We have discussed it enough.

Key Message
When your results meet your effort, keep the pedal to the metal and increase your efforts.

The Wall

This is almost like a real wall, made from bricks and mortar and of course, very solid. Just imagine you have hit this wall. You didn't expect it to be there, but there it is lurking behind a blind bend. The odd thing about this wall is this; it wasn't there yesterday when you travelled along the same road. I mean, what idiot built this thing overnight and fancy putting it in such a stupid place! None the less you have just run slap bang into it.

How suddenly would you come to a stop?

What would it feel like?

What would the emotional jolt be like?

What could you do about it?

How would you react?

In fact jot down your answers right now to these questions and then review them after you have finished the chapter.

The first four points are totally irrelevant in our imaginary case because the wall has been well and truly walloped. It has happened and there is nothing you can do about it – this time!

The last point you can do something about. This is a very simple process that I have explained to thousands of people. Some get it immediately and some don't. The process is so simple. In fact, it is so simple it just may be profound. Now I am not accustomed to saying things that are profound so when I do, I ask my colleagues to tell me I have done it. In this way I can feel so much better!

It goes like this;

In life we all face a series of events. Often these events are outside of our control and sometimes we can either consciously or sub consciously create these events to suit our needs or games we are playing, usually with ourselves, at the time. For example

You are late for a train and you miss it

Someone crashes into your car whilst it is parked

A client changes their coaching provider unexpectedly and you lose the contract

You are made redundant

You get stuck in a traffic jam

Most of the above can been seen in everyday life somewhere across the country. Some are quite simple and silly, whilst others can be a little more serious. Of course, in comparison to an illness or the loss of a loved one they can pale into insignificance, except when they are happening to you. In that moment the event is likely to be the most terrible thing that could have happened, at the most inappropriate moment. Why? Because it is happening to you right here and right now!

What really matters in this situation are the choices you make, which in turn will determine the outcome. In other words, how you respond to this event is vital.

There are some automatic responses that are inbuilt, e.g. the fight or flight instant response to danger and so on. In simple terms this is an almost animal-like reaction to an event; a cat and a mouse, a dog and a lamp post or a hungry lion and an antelope. But I am not talking about this system at all. I am talking about choice.

The lion is hardly likely to think,

"Hey that antelope looks like Bambi. Saw the film, made me cry, think I will go vegetarian."

Unlikely I'm sure you will agree.

I am talking about choice, your choice that we as humans can make every day to any given event. We may not be able to control the event but we can determine how we respond to it.

Let us therefore take one of the examples we have already identified

You are stuck in a traffic jam

There are a number of things that are almost guaranteed to happen in this situation;

You can get angry at the world.
You get frustrated.
You blast the car's horn.
You blame someone, (anyone) for breaking down or having an accident.

You blame the people who decided to put road works in this silly place at this busy time.

And so on, and so on.

You know that all of the above will not get you out of the traffic jam and that these reactions are not helping you. The responses are then internalised and in the end only serve to make you feel even worse. You also know that you will now be late to see your very important client. This feels like the end of the world. However just ask yourself.

"Are the people I am about to meet human too?"
"Has this ever as happened to them?"

The chances are that it has, so relax. If you are genuine then the meeting can be rescheduled or they may agree to meet with you a little later.

The only time this is unlikely to work for you is if you have stayed in bed a little late, or had another cup of tea, then your feelings of guilt will make you feel as if it is your fault and of course, it is.

I am not saying always:

"Live in the present" or
"Make the best of a bad situation."

I am asking you to think about your choices in any situation, and to remember that you do have a choice about how you respond. Always!

My challenge to you, is that you choose a different response. Just notice your first thought, which may be the frustration and so on and then work on the second thought, the choice you are about to make to respond differently. You cannot physically move the traffic so what response can you have that leaves you feeling positive and in control. What if you had thought to carry some talking books or CDs on learning a new language? The time waiting is then well spent. These are things that I might do. And I understand they may not work for you. What is important is to consider what will work for you (not what someone else suggests or at worst tells you to do). Note your choices down and refer to them regularly.

After you have done this think about a real event that has recently happened to you and the choices you made about your response. Then identify what was the driver behind the choice. Now choose a different driver and notice how the response moves to a more positive outcome.

The diagram below might be helpful;

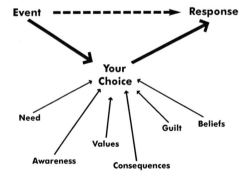

Note; the top line is the fight or flight response

All the above drivers that feed into the choices you make will lead to a different response. Of course as the driver is situational you may respond differently to the same event on a different occasion. The key question to ask if you feel you are acting out of character is;
"What has changed here, the event or my choice?"

I will share with you a personal example,

I was travelling by mainline rail to London to see a major client. The train stopped about 45 minutes from the destination; the guard came on the intercom and said,
"The power lines are down. We will be here for hours not minutes"

My initial reaction (my first thought) was the same as almost everybody else.

"Oh no. Not again. Now what?"

The guard now tells us,
"The train doors are open to allow passengers to make alternative arrangements or stretch their legs."

I have no idea how to get to my destination from where we had stopped. A bus. A taxi?

Many people were making calls to say,
"I won't be able to get to the office today because of a problem with the trains so I am going home"

This was their response to the event.

I decided I was going to London (my second thought). It was just a matter of how. I then overheard a woman asking her office to send a cab, so I simply asked her;
"Are you up for a cab share?"

She said she was and we left the train and waited. The cab turned up, we had a great journey. In fact, we discussed the different choices people were making and speculated why they did so. She was a very interesting person, who, as we reached London said that the cab would drop me right outside where I was going and when I offered my share of the fare she declined.

All I missed was one coaching session which was far more easily rescheduled than a whole day.

A different response may not have had such a positive outcome. Therefore what drivers do you think were impacting my choice? In this case it was all about my values and resilience.

Something to reflect on;

If I put a ten feet long, six inch wide plank on the floor, and asked you *"Can you walk across it?"* The chances are that you would answer *"yes"* and do it.

If I raised the plank onto two chairs and asked the same question. *"Can you walk across it?"* the chances are that you would.

If I placed the plank across the top of two fifty storey buildings and asked the same question. *"Can you walk across it?"* the chances are you would say. *"No I can't."*

Why is that? It is the same plank; it is still ten feet long and six inches wide. The plank hasn't changed at all. What has changed is the event; remember the event-response- choice mechanism. This change of event has brought into play a different driver which impacts your choice, maybe safety or survival.

The other thing that is likely to have changed is your focus. Instead of focusing on the end of the plank and success, you are looking at the drop. Therefore your focus is negative rather than positive. The use of this in building your business is simple. If you are feeling that you will never make it, just ask yourself what has changed. You are still the same positive and motivated person, so it is likely the event facing you has altered and therefore your choice on how you respond to it. Choose success.

Back to the wall, this usually kicks in around 3 months, that you are heading for is an imaginary one and is in my terms the realisation that you are actually running a business and having some success. You are engaged in a lot of activity which has culminated in proposals or propositions to prospective clients. Then suddenly you hit this wall that someone built overnight and your plans seem to go wrong.

You may lose your drive.

Maybe your activity drops away.

You don't seem to be able to communicate as well as you used to.

Your working practices become a mess.

Of course there are many other symptoms which I certainly don't want to implant in you.

Just stop.

This can and frequently does happen. Simply recognise it for what it is. A wall and that you have not lost the plot or forgotten what to do.

You are out there on your own, doing what you wanted to do and maybe dreamed of doing. This is now a reality and sometimes the reality can come as a shock. In addition Fred will pop up at this point just to compound the issue for you and confirm that he was right all along.

Just think about any event; now decide on your choice by picking the driver that will get you what you want. Remind yourself of the reasons you are doing this in the first place. Maybe you decided that it would be great fun to have your own business. Or maybe you had to overcome a personal obstacle to be a great coach. Business should be fun and if it isn't, ask yourself why not? Then having identified the reason, alter whatever it is that is making your business such a drag. Begin to have fun again. I said to a colleague of mine. *"You are spending too much time with people who keep telling you that you can't. Spend more time with people who will support you and tell you that you can."*

I often coach coaches on setting up their business and I recall one person who really hit the wall. The email I received said.
"I am all over the place at the moment. My communication is nowhere near as good as it was, I am not returning calls or emails. And what's more, my clients say they won't refer me as my charges are too low. I need a coaching session and I need it now."

I just emailed back with this response,
"So you have hit the wall, a little later than most people I must say. Remind yourself of your plan and who decides your fees. This is your business and your plan. What makes you think you need to change this because someone else has a different view? When do you want to talk?"

The reply was,
"I don't. The email did the trick. You are a genius."

Whist this is very complimentary, the fact is all I did was remind the coach of the event response mechanism and it unblocked the flow. So you can see how this can create awareness in you and for your business. This is also a great coaching tool to use with your clients.

Key Message
You can now prepare for the wall and go round it or through it if you prefer.

Chapter 11
New research

Survey of Executive Coaching in The City

A survey of coaching practices in The City in late 2005 has revealed that employers have access to very little reliable information on the subject of Executive Coaching.

Coaching is a relatively young industry which lacks formal standards. Because of this, around half of the decisions made on hiring coaches are based on referrals, according to findings from recruiter Morgan McKinley and Vicki Espin of Oxygen Coaching.

"Coaching refers to a vast array of activities from internal to external coaching and from life coaching through to executive coaching. There are currently no professional coaching standards as well as little or no regulation of the industry. Consequently, HR professionals have few guidelines to help them choose a coach or to measure the outcome of coaching." – Robert Thesiger, Morgan McKinley

The results of the survey are;

Q: What do you understand coaching to be?
   17% same as mentoring
   8% same as training
   4% another name for counselling and therapy
   4% the same as management consultancy

67% none of these – when pushed 40% of these respondents said it was more like mentoring

Therefore it would seem that whilst we think that coaching has become clear in buyers minds in terms of what it is, the survey indicates this is not the case.

Q: Do you currently use executive coaching?
70% yes
30% no

Q: What is executive coaching used for?
25% to enable key people to work on their own personal/professional development plans
23% to address specific issues
20% to enable people to continue to perform
15% to positively impact people's bottom line performance
9% to support formal training
5% other
3% as a perk

One of the biggest missed opportunities with regard to coaching is the failure to use it to support formal training.

Q: To whom is executive coaching offered?
8% Chairperson
12% CEO
22% MD
26% Directors
12% Middle Managers
20% other

Q: Do you internal and external coaches?
    50% external only
    12 % internal only
    38% both

Q: What selection process do you use?
    52% a strict selection process
    48% word of mouth or referrals

If almost half of the coaching opportunities are fulfilled through word of mouth then a coach's network and professional standards are vital.

Q: What criteria do you use when selecting an executive coach?
    27% coaches must be qualified
    14% coaches must have testimonials
    22% coaches must have a minimum length of experience
    23% coaches must be able to provide references
    14% other

Being qualified by a recognised institution is vital, however the survey shows that experience and testimonials play a significant part in gaining business in The City.

Q: How do you train your internal coaches?
    50% we use external trainers
    35% we use internal trainers
    15% we don't train them

Q: Do you measure the success of executive coaching?

54% yes

6% no it's too hard

6% it's not considered necessary

34% no don't know how to, we haven't found a method of doing this

40% of respondents would like to measure the return on their investment but just don't know how. In this book we have described how to maximise this key area. Until the coaching profession get to grips with this as a whole then the door is open to rogue coaches where the ROI may not be encouraged.

Q: How do you measure the success of executive coaching?

36% changes in behaviour

24% the reaction from person being coached

22% a positive change in the person's knowledge

12% impact on bottom line performance

6% other

This reflects the Kirkpatrick model of measuring success and will provide a good cornerstone for coaches to make a start on the measurement of success.

Q: Is coaching used strategically or ad hoc in your organisation?

64% ad hoc

36% strategically

In this book we have looked at how to align the objectives of the business with those of the line manager and the individual. More widely used, this framework will potentially remove the ad hoc approach seen in this survey.

Q: is coaching managed by HR or the Line?
76% HR
24% Line

Miss out the HR professionals at your peril.

Q: Over what length in months would a typical coaching intervention be?
24% 0-3 months
29% 3-6 months
22% 6-9 months
14% 9-12 months
11% 12 months +

Q: Are you planning to increase your coaching?
28% yes
22% no
50% not sure

This result is extremely positive. The 50% and 28% of respondents are prime targets for a coaching programme.

"God never had the time to make a nobody, only a somebody." – Mary Kay Ash

Chapter 12
"Right" said Fred

Just before we begin to answer the question, **"who is Fred?"** let me start by describing to you just where Fred comes from, where he lives and how he gets hold of information that he really needs to be able to talk to you.

In very simple terms we have 2 minds the conscious and the subconscious or unconscious, whichever you prefer.

For the purpose of this book I will use subconscious.

George Millar states that;
It is thought that the conscious mind can only hold about seven pieces of information, give or take a couple, at any one time and actively work on them.(I know that females think that the male brain can only hold one piece of information at any one time! This is clearly not true but I had better check it out!)

The subconscious on the other hand can hold untold amounts of information and some thinking is that it holds everything you have ever;

Seen
Heard
Smelt
Touched
Tasted
and so on, for your entire life.

Let's put this to the test. For example, have you ever smelt shoe polish and been immediately whisked back to your childhood? Or to your schooldays when you were at home with your parents?

Or have you ever entered an old fashioned grocery store and looked at the merchandise on the shelves, the large slabs of cheese or fresh pats of butter and remembered when you were young. Then let that warm feeling ease itself over you and maybe smiled to your self as the memories washed over you, so thick you could almost taste them. Or you hear a piece of music from your teens and the memories flash back to you in an instant. It's almost like a door swings open in your mind and you are back in time with the people and places you knew and loved. Your thoughts are maybe along the lines of, *"I can remember when..."*

This is our mind telling us, grass was greener, skies were blue and smiles were bright. Except of course when Fred is around and feeling very strong.

Fred is the name I give to my subconscious mind as you know by now and I can point exactly at the spot where he lives. It is that little bump on my skull just behind my right ear. This is Fred's home, in my head.

"Ok," I can hear you ask. *"Why on earth would you give a name to your own subconscious?"* The answer is quite easy. If I personalise this and give it an identity, then I can talk back to him whenever he enters into my life,

especially when I least expect him to, or when I don't need him.

No, I am not mad; it's a method I have spoken about for years to many people, both potential coaches, executive coaches and of course my own clients.

I can recall one woman who came up to me at a seminar I was speaking at and this is what she said;

"I have heard you speak before and I knew you were speaking here today so I just had to come. My husband brought me. I am not supposed to be travelling because I have just had a life saving operation. As I went down to the operating theatre on the trolley I was scared and anxious, yet all of a sudden I heard your voice saying to me, "It's just Fred in your head. It's just Fred in your head," and I started to laugh. So much so the anaesthetist wanted to know what was wrong. When I told him and the nurses they all started laughing as well. Then as if by magic it all seemed ok. I wanted you to know and to say thank you"

Thank you, was all I needed to say. However I was just completely lost for words. My reflection is, you never ever know what impact you may have on another when you say something that seems so simple to you, and yet it has a great impact on another person.

"When we do the best we can, we never know what miracle is wrought in our life or in the life of another." –
Helen Keller

Let's begin with what the subconscious is already holding that will either help or hinder you. Our sub conscious is where our belief system sits. We all have two main types of beliefs and whenever I have asked what these two main types are generally I hear the following answers:

Positive and negative
Good and bad
Right and wrong

The above are good answers and are absolutely correct for the people who gave them. I prefer to use two different ways of describing these beliefs. They are;

Empowering and limiting beliefs

The key question is which of these two are the strongest. No it's not the empowering beliefs. Although wouldn't we just love it if this were to be true? It is our own set of limiting or self limiting beliefs that are powerful. Let's give this a quick test;

I pose the following question and I want you to note down your immediate response. Be honest and don't change your mind.

You are 95% perfect, motivated and great at what you do;

Your immediate response was?
I bet maybe 98% or 99% of you had a response,
"Hey there, what about the 5% ?"

No matter how much I told you the 5% doesn't count and that it is not important, you just wouldn't let it go and would hound me until I gave you an answer. Of course, that would lead to a discussion about the things you didn't do so well and was a development need. This leaves me thinking. *"This isn't where I intended to go at all. I wanted to say just how good I thought you were. However the praise is now lost."*

What do you think is the reason for this thirst for the 5%? Rationally most people in any given situation, (e.g. at an appraisal, writing a report, carrying out a project) would settle for a score of 95% from the boss. None the less emotionally you seek that additional 5% that will make you perfect and give you that 100% score. You now know someone out there thinks you are not perfect and that you are missing 5% and then you have a burning desire to know what it is. Is it that you can't bear to think that somebody doesn't like you, or rates you less than perfect? Again you have a choice in how you respond. You can choose to let it go. Or if you must know, ask for clarity and evidence. In this way you can do something with the information. It is likely that the person you ask cannot quantify it which means

Feedback without evidence = opinion

Now will you let it go?
Who do you think this kind of comment feeds? You've got it in one. Fred and he is hungry for the 5% or the little remarks that don't serve you well. It's almost as if we

have a crapometer on our foreheads, like the Daleks' sink plunger, that sniffs out all this sort of information. By the very nature of it being a crapometer, it will not pick up any good news about you or anything positive or complimentary simply because it isn't programmed to do so. Believe me, your crapometer is sniffing around, just searching for anything that will prove what you always thought about yourself is actually true. In any event woe betide you that you should really hear and take in something positive, I mean it's just not the done thing, what!

An everyday occurrence that I am sure must have happened to you and only needs a two word answer and yet can turn into a whole debate in your head is this. Imagine you walk into a room and someone says:
"You look really smart today"

Our reply can be;
"As opposed to?"

What is the thought process going on behind this remark? You may assume it is a criticism of how you normally look; of course, right now, the chances are you are justifying this to yourself as humour!

Or;
"What, this old thing? I have had it for ages. It was the first thing I could lay my hands on this morning."

Ok! But who are you trying to kid?

This response is just a modesty defence mechanism.

The two words you need are, "thank you" and then shut up. You do not need to say anything else. Just accept graciously the compliments that come your way, store them and move on.

If a person's belief about themselves is that they are overweight, and will always be overweight. Even if they lost two stone in weight over a relatively short period of time, their belief mechanism kicks in again and just like an auto pilot the person's behaviours begin to change and the eating patters alter. Maybe to

One more chocolate biscuit won't hurt; well another one will be ok! Guess what? The weight comes back. This is called self sabotage or a self fulfilling prophecy.

Self belief is like a fragile little bird and can be crushed in a moment. Make sure your beliefs about yourself are positive and strong.

So, back to Fred. Remember the empowering and limiting beliefs?

I want to take a little time to look at where this stuff, (the limiting information and beliefs) comes from. Because that's all it is, just stuff! Also how it can, and does impact us, and how we can change things if we choose.

I am not intending to go into the psychological roots or

terms in this area, as there are many books on this. I want to look at this area in the way I have explained it to thousands of people, and at the same time, continue with the key theme of keeping it simple.

Life's lessons

So, here you are, a child in your most formative years, looking out at the world with a wide-eyed amazement and picking up everything you see, hear, smell, feel touch and taste. Of course you store it all in your sub conscious mind for later use, sometimes much later and yes your little crapometer has formed already and is working brilliantly. At this stage it is doing a good job. It is picking up information that you need to survive

Fred is also around, although you probably don't recognise him, but there he is. The strange thing is, Fred is someone you are likely to need. He is there to keep you safe. To let you know when you are in danger. He will pick up phrases such as;

- Don't go near the fire. It will burn you.
- Stop. Don't touch that it is hot.
- Walk, don't run
- The road is dangerous
- Don't talk to strangers. Tell a teacher
- Come straight home from school

And so on. All good and very necessary pieces of information. If a stranger appears Fred says to you;
"Don't talk to strangers. Where is that teacher? Run away."

When you are young these phrases and actions will keep you safe, however think about what impact they may have on you when you are an adult. Imagine this scenario;

Later in life, you are invited to a networking event, a place where the room is full of strangers. Except these are strangers you really need to talk to. That's one of the reasons you need to attend, but Fred kicks in with; **"Don't talk to strangers."**

He will be a bit sneakier about it now though and tell you in a very quiet way that is just enough to impact your behaviour. This is likely to be to run away. So the chances are that you won't go. However you will have a wonderful reason or self justification for not going. You may even get to the door and then turn back. The end result is just the same.

None the less, let's imagine that you make a positive choice and pluck up enough courage to go. To stay safe you may monopolise one person you already know or maybe the host. Of course you won't meet anybody else and the reason you give yourself for not meeting anyone else is cast iron. The event was badly organised and in any case there wasn't a single person who was a candidate for coaching. What a waste of time.

I think you know this just isn't true. What is probably true is that it's just Fred again mucking about with your head.

Fred is also picking up phrases and actions such as;

- Children should be seen and not heard.
- Don't be stupid now.
- How come you don't understand it is so simple?
- You are ranked and compared to other children which Fred hears.
- I give up you will never get this.
- You are as dull as dishwater.
- The bigger they are, the harder they fall.
- Sticks and stones will break my bones but names will never hurt me.

This simple childhood saying, of sticks and stones, that is often heard ringing out loud and clear in most school playgrounds, or from a parent to a child who is being called names. I now know that the saying is not true. A push or slap is far less damaging in the long term, than name calling. In my world the saying should be;

"Sticks and stones will break my bones today, but names can hurt me forever."

Some of the other phrases mentioned earlier can lead to;
- An introverted child and later in life an introverted adult.
- Someone who acts in a rebellious way to cover up the fact they think they don't understand.
- A really low responder. (Someone who doesn't speak out, or doesn't pro actively engage with others.)
- Someone who keeps themselves to themselves.
- Someone with low self confidence.
- Someone with a low self esteem.

These are the potential outcomes of just some of our childhood lessons, things that the crapometer has picked up and has given to Fred. He is no longer protecting you he is limiting you. You still need Fred but in a different way, so please let him know he needs a re-programme. More on how to do this later.

Taking a broader view of where Fred gets his fuel from;

Parents
Parent figures
Education
Friends
Religion
Media

Here is an example;
Young Elsie goes to a parent teacher's evening and is sitting listening to what is being said.

The teacher says,
"Elsie is great at most things but I have noticed she is slow in maths"

The parent says,
"Yes we have noticed that as well"

What has Elsie just become? Yes, slow at maths and now her crapometer is searching for any evidence, remarks or difficulties to prove the statements Elsie has just heard are true. This is known as a self fulfilling prophecy.

So what would a parent who is really self aware say? Or what would a coach say to the teacher? It may be;
"What do you mean by slow?"

or
"Compared to whom?"

or
"In what area of maths are you talking about specifically?"

Better still,
"What are you doing to help her?"
"What can I do to help her?"

Even better still,
"Tell me what Elsie is great at."

In this way you are now asking the teacher to feed Elsie with positives about the great things that the teacher swept away in their initial statement. Once this area is flowing and Elsie is glowing with pride, the specific questions you then ask about the subjects for development doesn't seem so bad and you are seen as an ally, along with the teacher, rather than feeding Fred. You see, he can't do anything other than store positives and what's more he cannot use this against Elsie later in life when she has to read a report and accounts as a part of her job.

I do some voluntary work at a local school , this work, which is great fun and a privilege, is tutoring year 12 students,(16-17 years) on how to coach year 8 and 9 students (13-14 years) with their studies and any issues that they may be facing that is hindering their progress at school. A forward thinking school. It's an absolute privilege and pleasure to work with these young adults. The influence that they will have now and will have in later years is enormous and this may help shape them in some way.

I was talking with the head of the maths dept: who instigated this initiative, about the scenario of a parent teacher evening. This is what he had to say.

"When I hear comments by parents saying we are worried about or notice that Johnny is not getting the marks we expect or that he is struggling with certain subjects, I think please don't say this, it is not where I want this to go. Not because it points a finger at me it's because I am looking for a positive recognition of what is going well!"

Another example I want to give you is the media. In particular advertising in any form: posters, magazines and television. I was listening to a very popular actress being interviewed and her standpoint was;

"The obsession we have with perfection in the human form is not healthy and goes against my deepest principles. That women should have perfect skin, hair and are all depicted as being a size eight, is being compounded by the celebrity magazines who print pictures in this way. Most if not all of them are airbrushed or even stretched to make the person look toned or thin-

ner, losing pounds in the stroke of a pen." She then went on to say. "This is just not reality and is especially dangerous to the health of teenagers." I was then stunned to hear her say, "I have to go on the covers of magazines and the airbrushing and touch up pen happens to me"

"Have to"? I thought. "No you don't. You choose to. You could say no, if it offends you so much. You are just giving theses magazines silent permission to continue." Refuse. Say "no, I won't do this and tell them your reasons." The point is this sort of promotion, picture or stimulus simply feeds into your Fred as you look at yourself in a mirror and make a comparison with the picture in front of you. Chances are, you end up thinking you are just not good enough thus compounding your limiting beliefs. Males face similar issues; we all have to have six packs, smooth skin and a full head of well-groomed hair.

By the way, did you know that unless you drink a certain brand of coffee you won't get a life partner? If you don't wash your clothes in a certain powder or liquid you will get talked about because your clothes are not white. The only people who go to slimming clubs are already slim, toned and laugh gaily whilst drinking a glass of wine.

Advertising plays to our deepest fears of not being good enough and that in some way, our life will be just a little short of perfect unless we buy a product. This must work otherwise why would the industry spend billions doing it? Personally, I like the ads that say, "Here it is. It does this. It's great. Buy it. See you!"

These messages telling us we are less than perfect are bombarded at us every single day. It's a field day for Fred who can gorge himself silly on all the things you haven't got.

Here is what two of my clients, who trained to be coaches, said about their inner limiting beliefs.

"Working with someone familiar with coaching was quite daunting and initially affected my coaching as I was conscious of how I might measure up to a good coach. As soon as I recognised the internal dialogue I could switch it off."

Another said,
"By nature I am a very confident individual, but was very concerned that my lack of practice in my new chosen career would be apparent with my first few clients. This affected my confidence internally as my inner voice kicked in. Although I believe it wasn't noticeable externally"

This is how the internal dialogue can work and not serve you well. It's just Fred who has picked up every thought you have had and is replaying them to you. This is how he pops into your world in real terms and if you just think about it for a moment. When do you think Fred is likely to talk to you the most? The chances are it will be;

- When you are about to do something new.
- When you face a new challenge.
- When you are feeling a little low.
- When you stand up to speak.
- When you are on your own.
- In the wee small hours of the morning, that 3am self doubt when things can and often do look bleak.
- If you are feeling a little down.

And so on

What is the answer to this? There are a couple of techniques that I use when Fred is at his most vocal and without even so much as an invite, pops into my head at the most inappropriate time. I am going to recommend them to you. The very first thing to do is to notice the thought and recognise it for what it is and who it is. If you then immediately talk back to Fred by telling him to, "delete" the limiting phrase, and replace the negative or limiting thought with something positive that will empower you. The most effective way to do this is to use 4 Ps.

The 4 Ps stand for,

Positive
Present Tense
Personal
Possible

This means you will make your response in a way that removes the first thought. It's just like pressing the delete key on your PC. In fact if you can imagine this action then it may well be even more effective.

So you just say out loud – "Delete."

Imagine you have just created a hole in Fred; you now need to fill this void with something that will serve you well and will empower you. This is where the 4 Ps come into play.

For example, let's have a look at a simple phrase that I would guess most people who are striking out on their own for the first time have, at some point, heard themselves thinking;
"I can't possibly work for myself."

Your objective is to change this thought to something that fits the 4Ps.

Positive

At first glance you may think that you simply replace the words,
I can't, with I can, i.e. I can work for myself.

However Positive and Present don't seem to fit, therefore you can make a much more meaningful change by altering I can and incorporate the Present tense.

This may now look like,
"I am"

Then you need to make it Personal, to get your own attention and focus and to ensure you notice the re pro-

gramme. Fred cannot pretend you mean this thought for someone else and by his very nature he takes it in.Therefore taking all the above into account this simple limiting phrase of,
"I can't possibly work for myself."

Turns into
"Elsie (your name here) I am working successfully for myself right now"

> Positive
> Present Tense
> Personal.

The chances are when you start this Fred will immediately reply,
"Yeah right! Who are you trying to kid?"

Do not agree with him. Just stick with your commitment to yourself and repeat the process again and again. You may of course not be working for yourself at the moment you start to use this re programme, but just think about your chances of success when you are. If you believe you can your chances have just gone up by a considerable amount.

Possible simply means that it really isn't much use saying "I am ten feet tall right now". This is not possible physically although it is possible to feel ten feet tall!

I realise that for some people the leap from 'I can't' to 'I am' may seem huge. So instead of setting yourself up to fail, set yourself up to succeed. You may decide to take a middle step and use;

"I am enjoying developing my business"
"I am learning how to develop my business"

"I am developing myself as a business person"

Then once you are comfortable with this you can then move to;
"I am working successfully for myself right now"

It's never too early to think positive thoughts about yourself.

> If you think you are beaten, you are.
> If you think that you dare not, you don't.
> If you'd like to win but think you can't,
> It is almost certain you won't
> If you think you'll lose, you've lost.
>
> For out in the world you'll find,
> Success begins with a fellow's will,
> It's all in a state of mind
> If you think you are out classed, you are.
> You've got to think high to rise.
> You've got to be sure of yourself before,
> You can ever win a prize
> Life's battles don't always go,
> To the stronger or faster man.
> But sooner or later the man who wins,
> Is the man who thinks he can.
> *Author unknown*

A re-programme may take some time and effort. Research shows that to complete a re programme you need to say your positive affirmation approximately ten times three times a day for 30 days before it becomes a reality, or you know that you are able to do exactly what you want.

In other words you 'act as if', or you 'fake it till you make it'.

"To establish yourself in this world do all you can to seem established already." – Francois, Duc de la Rochefoucald (1613-1680).

I will share with you a personal example and I would like you to spot the mistakes that I made.

I decided to learn the guitar, just to bash out a few sing along songs. I bought a guitar and I really struggled as I tried to get the hang of it. I bought some teach - yourself guitar books, and after trying to play this guitar, I realised it had to be the wrong guitar. Naturally I bought a more expensive one and I booked some lessons; this is more like it eh! Off I went to try and play this guitar. Then it struck me, it had to be the guitar, again! I saw a black model with pearl inlay. I had seen Neil Diamond playing one like it therefore I must be able to play one too.

The guy in the shop asked me,
"What do you want to be able to do?"

I gave him my original objective, he said,
"In that case this is the one for you and it's not expensive either."

I took it away and tried to learn to play this one. Failure, until I recalled the affirmation of

Positive, Present Tense, Personal and Possible. Therefore my focus became;
"Neil, I am playing this guitar right now."

As I picked up the guitar my whole attitude towards playing had changed it became fun and easier. This motivated me to practice more and I had it.

The mistake I made was thinking about the words try or trying. By removing these words and adding the 4Ps, I achieved my objective.

In coaching whenever you hear your client say, "I will try," challenge them. It means they won't. In coaching a commitment means they either will or they won't. Try just doesn't exist. My theory is simple. You cannot jump a ten feet gap, seven feet today and three feet tomorrow. It's all the way or not at all.

Back to our example;
"Elsie I am working for myself successfully right now" ***will help you; all you need to do now is do it.***

Your process now is to use the 4Ps and take action, which will re programme Fred.

"It's not enough to say Britain is best 3 times a day after meals and expecting it to be so. We have to work at it." – HRH The Duke of Edinburgh

I find the really sad thing is that as soon as you have a new, empowering and positive thought the change has already taken place. The trouble is you just don't believe it, because it can't be this simple. But it is. All that is happening is Fred is currently much stronger than your new affirmation. Just keep at it. Your reality is not as solid as you think.

There are a number of practical exercises that you can do to help you to really understand just how to begin to look at this reality. If you choose to do them for yourself and feel the benefits then you will be able to use them with any clients who are facing similar issues with Fred.

This is what I want you to do;

Take a clean sheet of paper or a notebook you can carry with you and over a period of two weeks write down all the things you tell yourself that don't serve you well. In other words, write down all your limiting thoughts.

Important note; if you have already completed a re programme, you may choose not to do this. I wouldn't want you to remind yourself of the things you have already removed.

Once you have completed your list, put a mark next to the belief that has the biggest impact on you.

Then ask yourself just one question,
"What hard evidence or proof do I have that the thought I have noted is actually true?"

Hard evidence means fact; it does not mean that you heard somebody say it, or that you seem to remember something about this from a long time ago, but hard evidence.

The chances are, as you do this you will smile to yourself, shrug your shoulders or even get upset. The plain facts from having done this many times are that the majority of you won't have any evidence at all. This means that something that has been bugging you for goodness knows how long is just not true. Sure you can concoct a wonderful story to yourself about why it is true. Just remember this is your justification to yourself about why you are the way you are. Be strong and determined to be a different you, if that's what you really want. Once this realisation has hit home you know what to do next. That's right;

Say *"Delete,"*
Positive, Present Tense and Personal affirmation.

Take Action.

I did have one guy say to me at a seminar I was speaking at;
"I have some hard evidence Neil. I am black. That's hard evidence and it limits me."

My reply was very straightforward,
"Yes you are black. I can see that. However that is not the thing I want you to think about. What I want you to do is ask yourself how does this impact you? What is the tangible outcome? What does it stop you from doing? Then deal with that."

He was truly amazed at my response and the different way of thinking about what he thought was insurmountable. He came up to me afterwards and said, "You are the first person who has challenged me on this in this way. I expected you to skirt around the horny issue of my skin and you didn't. Thank you."

Another example is a woman, who said to me,
"I am fat. Everyone can see that and this is hard evidence."

Of course my first challenges to her were,
"Who is everyone?"
"Compared to whom?"

After she had taken a moment to process the challenges, I could see her begin to question her belief. Then I asked her;
"How is this impacting you? What does it stop you doing" Let's deal with that."

My next challenge was, *"What do you want instead?"*

This was followed by clarifying some goals and options around how she would deal with this new perspective.

One final thought is for you, the coach. Your client, who is working on a positive affirmation, will benefit enormously if you challenge their affirmation with a very direct response. All I want you to say after they have said their affirmation out loud is,

"I don't believe you," and ask the client to say it again and again until you do believe them. It really is not enough just to say the words; we need the client to say it with every fibre of their body. In their tone, body language and in their eyes. Most people can fake a smile or tone or even body language but my firm belief is they cannot fake what is in their eyes. So watch them closely as they tell you what they are thinking. You will see the truth in the windows to their soul, their eyes.

If you are doing this exercise for yourself then here is my challenge,

"I don't believe you. Say it again."

Just remember when you think you can't, or you have given up on you, a great coach will think you can and will never give up on you.

Take a 7 day detox
Alter your focus from negative to positive. Sounds easy? Ok try this.

Create a two column table.
In the left hand column write down everything you hear yourself say internally and externally that is negative.

In the right hand column write down everything you say internally and externally that is positive.

Study the lists and focus on the positive.

For seven days every time you think something or are about to say something negative, reframe it to positive or do not say anything at all.

If you do say something negative or linger internally on a negative you have to start the seven days all over again.

That's right it's a rolling seven days. So if you get to day six and say something negative then you start again for another seven days.

This will alter your focus from negative to positive. Oh and by the way this includes gossip.

One final exercise you may wish to do is this.

Do this exercise quickly. Take your list of limiting beliefs and draw a box around them. Take a pen and with your most positive flourish strike a line through them from a top corner to a bottom corner.

Write along the line,
"Delete."

Then underneath write,
"This is the way I used to be."

You have just pressed the delete key, not on a single

item, but a whole package of things you don't want in your life or your inbox.

Now you need to replace this with something positive that you do want.

Take a clean sheet of paper, and write down everything and I mean everything that you are great at, without editing and without modesty. Then once you have finished give it to your partner or a close friend and explain what you are doing and how important it is to you. Ask them to add to the list. Then ask your children if you have them or other friends and ask them to do the same. Then find someone else that you love and trust outside the family group and ask them to add to it By the end of this exercise, you will have stacks of evidence that you can feed into Fred which is positive and written out with thought. Keep the papers or notebook and the next time you have a down day take it out and read it. Really understand how much thought and love went into completing the lists for you. Then allow yourself and give yourself permission to feel great, and remember;

What matters the most is how you see yourself.

You are not looking to remove Fred completely. He is also there to keep you safe or to ring alarm bells. As one client said to me.
"If the squirrels are out of the box (his Fred) then there is either something I am not comfortable with or a decision that needs revisiting. The difference is, now I can

tell the difference between safe and self limiting messages."

You are looking to re programme Fred to give you positive thoughts about yourself. In fact you can ask Fred only to give you positive messages and just like the genie in the bottle, the reply will be;
"Your wish is my command."

I said earlier there are two ways of dealing with this; the second depends on your point of view, scepticism and beliefs. You can just ask the universe for what you want. You can just know that you will be successful and people will come. To explain what I mean, I was driving along a motorway to visit a client and my thoughts wandered into thinking about a colleague I had, who had set up a business and I wondered how he was getting along as we hadn't been in touch for years. At that precise moment the phone rang and it was him. We caught up as if we had seen each other yesterday (on hands free) and he asked me if I was still into executive coaching and if so did I want an assignment with a CEO of a Global company, as he didn't specialise in coaching. You bet I did.

So was this a coincidence or was it something else? You decide. There is just one thing to remember about this, the Universe rewards action and this book is about our thoughts and, so either way you win!

All I will say is;
"Be careful what you ask for because you just might get it.

Chapter 13
Appendices

The Price is Right – Solution

If you completed the pricing exercise you will of course have an answer.

Whatever that answer is, you would have, or would not have been, able to deliver a programme to the required specification. You may have come up with a solution that the client would have bought. However would it have generated the desired outcome and revenue for you?

I will tell you what happened step by step.

A power point presentation was prepared with bound print outs for the attendees.

The power point was used at the start of the presentation. Then I asked if we could stop using power point and just discuss the programme I had in mind and what the organisation really wanted. Much to their relief (they had already been power pointed to death) it was agreed. I deliberately chose spot number three. The logic behind this was;

I believed I could impress them enough to be better than the first two presentations, you just need self belief. Then all I needed to do was to set a standard that the last presentation of the day had to beat (my bet was there would be another power point show).

By asking a number of questions the feedback I initially gave to them was;

"You can't effectively do what you want for the budget you have set. Well you can but in my experience it wont work."

"Where did you get the 20k from in the first place?" (Remember this programme supports a multi million pound initiative.)

They replied,

"It seemed like a good number but we don't have an idea that is set in stone."

I asked,

"What would happen if we could ignore the investment for the time being?"

They said,

"Show us what you would do"

I went over to the flip chart and we designed an outline programme that I could recommend and that would be successful. They accepted that what we had discussed and agreed together would work and that they liked it.

The last presentation was not successful and we got the contract. The programme we delivered was;

1. Meet with the senior management team for a day and decide,

- What the outcomes would be?
- What it would be like once the programme had been delivered?
- What culture the organisation wanted?
- What the measures of success would be?

2. Run the first 2 day workshop for the directors on "Coaching for Success." Using 2 CECO coaches per course.

3. Take the top 40 managers through a 2 day course 10 at a time - 4 courses

4. Take the training team through the 2 day course as participants.

5. Run a 1 day followed by 2 day "Train the Trainer" programme for the trainers.

6. Co – facilitate with each trainer to ensure they could run the programme.

7. Sign off the trainers or complete additional training to enable sign off to take place.

8. Mark all participants' portfolios to accredit the managers and directors as internal coaches.

9. Attend the presentation evening (where accreditation certificates were awarded) and deliver a key note speech.

10. Running alongside the main programme provide 1-1 coaching for the directors.

11. The organisations trainers then roll out the programme to the rest of the organisation.

Once this was completed we were then asked to design a Master Class Programme to take managers to the next level of coaching skills.

As you can imagine this programme on the example fees we have used was well in excess of the original £20,000 budget.

Sometimes you just need to be bold. The organisation is expecting you to be the expert in this area and to make recommendations. Ask yourself what is the worst that can happen? In truth you win a contract for £20,000 and that is not so bad is it? As long as you have pointed out to the organisation there are alternatives which may be outside of their initial budget.

Of course, you have to believe there is an alternative in the first place!

"What we think or what we know or what we believe is, in the end, of little consequence. The only thing of consequence is what we do." – John Ruskin

Suggested Reading List forExecutive Coaches

The Coaching Manual
Julie Starr
ISBN: 0-273-66193-0

Coaching for Performance
John Whitmore
ISBN: 1-85788-303-9

Time To Think
Nancy Kline
ISBN: 0-7063-7745-1

Co-Active Coaching
Laura Whitworth, Henry Kimsey-House, Phil Sandahl
ISBN: 0-89106-123-1

Executive Coaching with Backbone and Heart
Mary Beth O'Neill
ISBN: 0-7879-5016-5

The Inner Game of Work
Timothy Gallwey
ISBN: 1-84203-015-9

Working with Emotional Intelligence
Daniel Goleman
ISBN: 0-7475-4384-4

MBA Management Models
Sue Harding & Trevor Long
ISBN: 0-566-08137-7

Games People Play
Eric Berne
ISBN: 0-14-002768-8

Extracts Taken From the Film Rudy

This extract is taken from the true story of Daniel. E. (RUDY) Reitteger.

Rudy had a burning ambition and drive to play American football for Notre Dame College, 'The Fighting Irish'. Here are some extracts from his story.

We begin the story with Rudy at about 8 years of age; he plays football with his brothers and friends. He is the smallest kid on the block and although he is passionate he gets knocked about quite a lot.

When Rudy shares his dream with his family they laugh at him. His father says, "Rudy. Notre Dame is for rich kids, smart kids, not people like us."

His father works at the local steel mill and says to Rudy *"You will make a living at the plant and if you work hard you will make a better living at the plant than I have."*

His high school take a field trip to Notre Dame and Rudy signs up to go. Just as he is getting on the bus his teacher says. "Where are you going, you haven't got the right grades and you will not get into Notre Dame" and he turns Rudy back.

So Rudy starts his job at the plant. On Rudy's 18th birthday, Peetie, his best friend gives him a jacket he bought from a pawn shop. It's a green and gold Notre Dame jacket. Rudy puts it on and Peetie says *"you were born to wear that jacket"*. But Rudy continues to work at the plant for four years.

Then Peetie dies in an accident at the plant. This makes Rudy think again about his dream which just will not die and he decides to do something about it. He decides he will go to Notre Dame.

Remember, Rudy is about 5-8" and weighs in at about 11stone wet through. He wants to play with giants, huge guys who dwarf him and on top of that, he does not have the grades to get into Notre Dame.

He has saved $1000 which he uses to go to Notre Dame. He arrives at 3-00am and persists with the gate security until he finally gets to see a priest. Rudy says to the priest.

"Ever since I was a kid I wanted to come here. Ever since I was a kid everyone said it couldn't be done. My Parents, my teachers, my brothers, my friends everyone, except Peetie. My whole life people have been telling me what I could and couldn't do, and I used to believe them. I don't want to do that anymore."

Initially the priest thinks Rudy wants to become a priest. However Rudy soon puts that right and persists until the priest says. *"OK. Here is the deal. Holy Cross is nearby. I can get you 1 semester. If you make the grades you may get a second and then maybe, just maybe, you have a chance of getting into Notre Dame"*

Rudy then went to the Notre Dame football coach and says to him. *"I will play for Notre Dame and I wanted to introduce myself to you, so you will know who I am when I get here."* Remember he isn't even in Holy Cross yet.

What about that for a positive affirmation and belief in himself?

Rudy does get into Notre Dame and a friend helps him keep up with his studies. He also gets into the football squad. During all his time there he never misses one single practice, but he never gets picked to play. Rudy however has gained huge admiration and respect from his team mates through his heart and dedication.

Just before the last game, in his last year at Notre Dame the team captain goes to the football coach and says. *"Coach. I want Rudy to dress in my place"* and puts his football shirt on the desk. The coach says, *"Don't be ridiculous, you are an all American and captain of this team, act like it."* The captain says. *"I believe I am."*

Every single player without exception comes into the office and they all say. *"I want Rudy to dress in my place"* and they put their shirts on the coach's desk. So the coach picks Rudy to play. Rudy phones his family and his friends hear about him being picked so they turn up to see him play. But the coach doesn't send him on to the field.

The team decide this isn't right and agree to disobey the coaches instructions and make a specific play with about 10 seconds to go which will bring on the defence. This means Rudy. At the same time the other members of the team start a chant of RUDY- RUDY- RUDY. The crowd pick this chant up and slowly one by one, then by the dozen and eventually all the people in the stadium start the same chant without really knowing why.

The coach sighs and sends Rudy on to play with only 10 seconds remaining of the last ever game he can play. His mother cries *"He looks so little."* His friend who helped him with his studies yells. *"Who is the champ now?"*

He makes a tackle, which has no bearing on the result of the game as it is already won. But, it is a massive moment for the players, his friends, and his family. Rudy has finally achieved his dream. He played football for Notre Dame.

Since 1975, Rudy is the only player ever to be carried off the pitch shoulder high by his team mates. Rudy goes on to graduate from Notre Dame, which he almost sees as a by product. Five of his younger brothers go to college and they graduate.

The question I ask you is.

"How many lives did Rudy change?"

"How many lives did the priest change?"

"How many lives did Peetie change? and he never knew." (or did he)

I think they all changed so many people's lives. How can we measure the impact of Rudy on countless others? One man who had faith in himself and discarded the limiting beliefs that were being tossed at him from every direction.

I believe Daniel. E. (RUDY) Reitteger is truly inspirational.

An incredibly powerful story about the strength of the human spirit.

An interview with Neil Espin (the Author)

A colleague of mine was carrying out some research into why people love their jobs and what makes them tick.

I was asked if I would do the interview and I agreed. This is an extract.

Q: What inspires you?
It's the hearts and mind stuff that really gets to me. I feel I can do anything when something that touches this nerve comes my way.

For Example;

Quotations of all types for example.

"If" by Kipling

"The credit belongs" Theodore Roosevelt

"Sunscreen" Baz Lurman

Also all kinds of music and books

Certain films, I really like true stories or feel good factor films such as.

"Rudy" – of course.

"Field of Dreams" – A simple Iowa farmer who has the course to follow his dreams. A voice in his field says "If

you build it he will come" these were the first words he heard. He followed his dream.

"If you build it he will come"

"It's a Wonderful Life" – It's a classic Christmas tale with many threads running through it.

"When a bell rings an angel gets their wings'

"Regarding Henry"- which all workaholics must see – Never put work before your life, here is a story of a tough, hard working lawyer who gets a second chance. A chance to put things right.

"As soon as you have had enough you say – when!"

"Men of Honour" A true story of one mans battle against racial prejudice to fulfil his destiny. He is helped along the way from a most unexpected source.

"Step up to the line cookie and give me twelve"

"The Natural" – A story about Roy Hobbs. A truly great baseball player who looses his way and eventually finds his path into the record books.

"I wanted to be the greatest baseball player that ever lived" And then what?

"Rocky 1" The film itself is based on a true event, the Ali v Wepner fight. The inspiration is about Sylvester Stallone. He had nothing and even sold his dog Butkiss

to pay the rent. Stallone saw the fight and wrote Rocky. Stallone had such overpowering self belief that he would write and star in his film. Hundreds of studios turned him down. Eventually he settled for a small cash amount and a take of the box office. Rocky grossed $200million.

"I aint going down no more"

"Coach Carter" A true story based on successful basketball player turned coach who takes on an underperforming high school team. The coach puts education alongside results on the court with an amazing outcome.

"What are your deepest fears?"

"Remember the Titans" – A true story about a black American coach placed in charge of the first multi racial football team. The way this man and his team overcome this huge barrier and a town is awe inspiring.

"Before we turn to hate, we always remember the Titans"

"Hidalgo" – A true story about one man and his horse. Showing how heart can be more important than size or wealth.

"Mister, no one hurts my horse"

"The Worlds Fastest Indian" - A true story showing that age has no bearing on fulfilling a dream.

"I always wanted to do something big"

Other things are; the natural world and in particular, the seashore and the wind in my face.

In business terms a person who has that 'aha' moment and they say to me,

"That has changed the way I see this issue. I can do this".

Q: What motivates you?
My values. These are my true motivators, the things that get me up in a morning. The things I want to be, more than things I want to have.

Q: How do you sustain your level of motivation?
I firmly believe in doing what I say I will do. Working with people as unique individuals without judgement or prejudice. Acting fairly and honourably, treating people with respect regardless of position or the role they have in life. I need to know that I make a difference to each person I touch. By asking for feedback I receive the answers to this question. This enables me to be better at what I do and therefore be a more effective person in life and business.

I have deleted completely from my thinking the phrase *"the end justifies the means."*

I know that when I consistently act in this way, then my level of motivation is maintained.

Q: What challenges it?

Primarily it's the travelling I do. The long drives, motor-ways and endless traffic jams. Train journeys and the delays. I get over this by owning a nice car and travelling 1st class. This is not a status thing at all. I do this for me, my peace of mind and to maintain strength in my own inner self.

I find that watching leaders of organisations who act as though people don't matter really demotivates me. However I know that through my job I can help people to see that there is a different way to achieve aims and objectives without a disregard for other people's lives.

Q: What do you see as the most important aspect of remaining inspired / motivated?

When I am in this frame of mind, I feel good, my life is better and my impact on others is far more positive. It wouldn't really do if one of my clients said to me, *"I have had a really tough time and I want to talk it through"* and I replied,

"You think you have had a raw deal? Listen to my day."

This ultimately means I am not an energy vampire.

Q: Who inspires you?

This is a tough one to answer.

The universe inspires me, I just know that all is well up there and I am still amazed at the opportunities that it sends me.

On a practical note, I do some voluntary coaching in schools with the 16/17 year old students. They inspire me. When I consider all the possibilities that lay before these young people are so amazing and some of them do not recognise it. But there I am being given a chance to open a door in their minds to these possibilities. I then watch and listen to their reactions to a different way of thinking about things. This is an absolute privilege.

Of course when I work with other coaches and certain clients, they also inspire me to do more and sometimes to think differently.

The upshot is; I also look for my own inspiration inside myself.

Q: Who do you consider to be outstanding role models?
My initial reaction is – I don't have any- I have thought about it, considered it and I have come to an amazing conclusion – I don't have any.

Q: Do you have any heroes? Who?
I want to answer this question initially from the world of sport.

Mohammed Ali, Seve Ballesteros, Jimmy Greaves, Brian Clough, George Best.

These are all people who have a natural ability, they are not mechanical and they are not always technically brilliant. They just seem to flow. I really admire people who can go out and do it rather than just write about it.

I met some Battle of Britain fighter pilots and they were old boys as you can imagine. That was an experience I am unlikely to repeat. They had just a humble acceptance of a job that needed to be done and they did it. Laughing and reflecting, I imagine, as they each in turn signed my print of a Spitfire. I still have it to this day.

On that note my father was 16 years old, a Royal Marine and on Russian Convoys in 1942. Whilst I never thought of him as a hero, he was. I never told him.

Q: When you were a child, what did you think you'd be when you grew up?
When I was a boy I thought I would work in a factory as an engineer like my father and his father. But I wasn't that clear to be honest. As I moved into my teens that changed, I wanted to be a commercial artist or a forest ranger. However our careers master hadn't heard of these things so I was left with the normal, Civil Service or The Forces. I didn't really fancy the Civil Service so I decided to join the Royal Navy and applied to the officer training college. I just needed to sign and I was in. I don't know why but I didn't. I think I found girls!

I then realised I could communicate really well and that I did not want a trade. So, I just wrote to all the firms that dealt with our local village store and got a job with a textile firm. My intention being to work my way up through the various roles in the organisation and eventually I would become a sales representative.

Q: What advice would you give to others on how to be really well inspired / motivated?

In simple terms. Decide what you want to be in life, rather than what you want to have. The first is trickier than the second. However, get the 1st right, commit to yourself that you will be who you are, rather than whom you are not. In other words become your true self in life and don't play act. And the rest follows.

Never wait for someone else to take responsibility for your future. Experience shows me that no matter how well intentioned that person may be they will never be as passionate about your life as you will. Many people have come to me for coaching and have huge disappointments, having placed their dreams and ambitions in the hands of another without actually taking responsibility themselves.

Be aware that it is never too late to be what you want to be.

Q: Could you / would you say what your main priorities in life are?

I can and I will. I want freedom and health for my wife Vicki and myself, along with all that goes with it. I also have the same wish for family.

Always put people before things.

Q: How do you perceive the role of the leaders these days?

I think that in today's world the modern leader, the

informed and insightful leader is the one who believes in the potential of people. Certainly role modelling is vital; Nine times out of ten, staff will take their lead from the organisation's leaders and adopt the observed behaviours for themselves. Therefore a phrase I often use is one that gives leaders a taste of stark reality.

"When you look out into your organisation, what you see is a direct reflection of who you are."

If.

If you can keep your head when all about you
are losing theirs and blaming it on you.
If you can trust yourself when all men doubt you,
but make allowances for their doubting too.

If you can dream and not make dreams your master.
If you can think and not make thoughts your aim.
If you can meet with triumph and disaster,
and treat both those impostors just the same.

If you can bear to hear the truth you have spoken
twisted by knaves to make a trap for fools.
And watch the things you've given your life to broken,
and stoop and build them up with worn out tools.

If you can make one heap of all your winnings,
and risk it on one turn of pitch – and – toss.
And lose, and start again at your beginnings,
and never breathe a word about your loss.

If you can force your heart and nerve and sinew,
to serve your turn long after they are gone.
And so to hold on when there is nothing in you,
except the will that says to them, hold on.

If you can talk with crowds and keep your virtue.
Or walk with kings and not lose the common touch.
If neither foes nor loving friends can hurt you,
and all men count with you but none too much.

If you can fill the unforgiving minute,
with sixty seconds' worth of distance run.
Yours is the earth and everything that's in it,
and - which is more - you'll be a man my son.

"If"
Rewards and Fairies (1910)
Rudyard Kipling

The Credit Belongs

The credit belongs to those who are actually in the arena.
Who strive valiantly, who know the great enthusiasms,
The great devotions, and spend themselves in a worthy
cause.
Who at the best know the triumph of high achievements
and who, at the
worst, if they fail, fail while daring greatly. So that their
place shall never
be with those cold and timid souls who know neither
victory nor defeat.

Theodore Roosevelt

<u>Inspirational verse</u>

Leaders need to inspire people to be the best they can be and lead them towards a vision of what is possible. Integrate meaningful and defined values and behaviours. Always do the right thing, not follow processes and do things right. The latter will lead to mediocrity. When leaders get this wrong everyone notices. I believe this is best summed up by the following quote;

'A leader is best when people barely know he exists.

Not so good when people obey and acclaim him.

Worse when they despise him, fail to honour him.

But a good leader who talks little when his work is done,

His aim fulfilled, they will all say.

"We did this ourselves." '

Lao-Tsu – The Way of Life 604 BC

The Duel

The scene is set. Steely glares cross the room.
Weapons keen, one to win and one is doomed.
The hush descends. The clock ticks on.
Towards high noon.
Words slash across the void. Who will give?
Stand your ground if you want to live.
The stakes are high. The duel is on.
The thrust, the parry, first blood drawn.
The winner stands tall, proud of their skill.
The other one down, in for the kill.
Decision made, stroke of a pen.
That's another board meeting over then.

Neil Espin
From 1997
My time in Corporate Life

Be Larger than Life

"Hallo, Piglet. This is Tigger."
"Oh is it?" said Piglet and he edged round to the other side of the table.
"I thought Tiggers were smaller than that."
"Not the big ones," said Tigger.

A.A. Milne & E.H. Shepard

Printed in the United Kingdom by
Lightning Source UK Ltd., Milton Keynes
142535UK00001B/108/A